Sometimes our imagination
is better than the reality

I JUST IMAGINED

HANIYA KHUSHNOOD

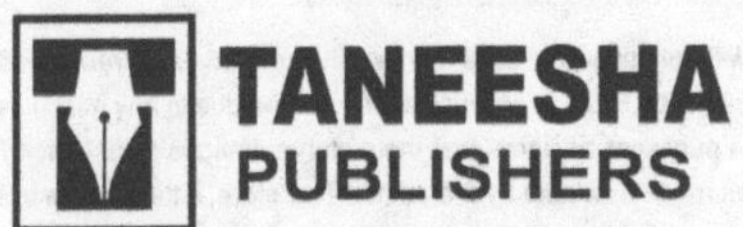

Title   :   I Just Imagined

Author   :   Haniya Khushnood

Edition   :   1st (May, 2023)

ISBN   :   9789390910915

Published by

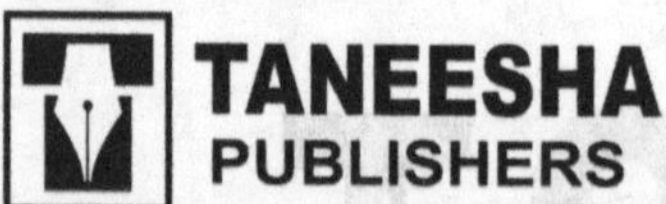 **TANEESHA PUBLISHERS** | *A Venture of -* **PRACHI DIGITAL PUBLICATION**

Regd. Add.: 254, Khuriyakhatta No. 10, Bindukhatta,
Lalkuan, Nainital - 262402, Uttarakhand, India
Website : www.taneeshapublishers.in
E-mail : info@prachidigital.in
Contact : +91-976041-7980, 845481-2712

Printed by :
Manipal Technologies Limited, Manipal - 576104, Karnataka

Introduction

This novel is actually really precious to me as this is my first novel I have written. There are few moments mentioned in the novel that really happened to me in real life and for me, it's personally really funny to read. When I came up with the storyline the first time, I was actually pretty impressed by myself.

I've actually been writing little stories and poems since I was seven years old. My dad gave me a white spiral notebook, and I was so happy at first. Then I started writing poems, not by myself, I started to copy them down from my school textbooks. After I lost interest in writing down useless things, I started to read story books. My uncles gifted me lots of storybooks, from which I actually learned about writing a lot.

Then I started to write poems and stories by myself, which I personally find so interesting. Then I suddenly got interested in journaling more.

When I was in my first teen year, I had to face lots of problems, which made that the hardest year of my life, at least till now. I had to deal with toxic friendships, social anxiety, weight gain, academic downfall and more. It had me losing my mind. Those months, all I did to pass my time was journaling hundreds of pages. Even though I tried to tell the people around me that I'm not weak, I'm trying my best, nothing worked. I was filled with negativity. But other people had only one thing to say, that it was all just my teenage years, and nothing serious.

But these heartbreaks really helped me getting into writing once again.

After that year, everything changed. It just proves that how time heals everything. Right now, I might be living the best time of my life, I healed through everything.

I am the quite kid in my class, who is an average student, has only one or two friends, and sits in the corner of the class, writing tons of pages filled with meaningful quotes. I used to get many compliments regarding my writings.

But once I got into reading real novels, and my uncle gave me a hope of writing my own novel, I started one.

If everything goes well, there will another novel coming soon.

I really hope ya'll like this book, which is not filled with lots of plot twists, but an interesting life, with a sad back story.

Sage

Even though they say that time heals all wounds, the scars are still freaking there. I can't forget what happened. I can't forget how I felt.

I stood they're in front of the water on the beach, no one else there, just me, and those memories. The water was flawless and sparkling with the light of the moon, as I just sobbed there.

"YOU'RE UNBELIEVABLE AMY" I just yelled it and tried to let it all out. I couldn't take it anymore. My head was hurting so bad, it felt like it will explode.

I wanted to punch something, *or someone,* so bad. The mental pain was killing me from inside. I was about to scream another sentence when someone pulled my arm from behind.

"What are you doing here? Why are you letting that past person destroy the present you Sage?" she pulled me in for a hug.

It was my cousin, Blair.

I immediately hugged her back with my face all wet with my tears. I just want to forget Amy and focus on my present but it's been really difficult for me and I don't know what to do or how to react on things.

Isn't it crazy how people have only a sentence about you in their lives, while you have a whole chapter about them?

"Hey, it's really late now, and tomorrow is the first day of your new life, lets go home" Blair stated, pulling me out of the hug and looking me in my teary eyes. I just nodded and moved along with her. I drove here to the nearest open place with the water view. I didn't notice she followed me.

This is my favorite place to come when I have a mental breakdown. I was feeling really burned out, but I didn't knew I could break out crying so bad. I just got these sudden memories of Amy, after years.

I am new to Texas, and I just moved in with my two cousins, Blair and his brother Trevor. I'll be helping them with running their newly opened restaurant from tomorrow, hopefully. It's a fortune that us three are all in our twenties together. Me and Blair are the same age and Trevor is just an year old.

I tugged myself in my bed, and I just wanted to switch off my mind, forget every single thing that has happened to me back in Ohio.

I had a nice and consoling sleep then.

I woke up with sun rays on my face. "Oh come on are you serious, it's not really refreshing, it's annoying, I just want another ten minutes please" I mumble to myself.

Oh wait, I'm employed now.

Damn it, I had to wake up to get ready for my first day at work. I can't wait to go back to Ohio to meet my parents. That's kind of stupid how I just came her a few days ago and already thinking about visiting my parents. When am I going to grow up?

I slowly roll out of bed. No wait, I really mean it, I *roll* out of my bed, and fell to the ground. Trevor walks in my room, and saw me and my blanket down on the floor.

"What the hell are you doing down there" he looked at me confused, as if I was a frog. I was embarrassed but I didn't care.

"Do you ever know how to knock?" I asked him standing up. He rolled his eyes, leans on the door and said "I'm not used to knock and come; this is the first time we have a guest come over to our house".

"Well get used to it because I'm gonna be here for a very long while, so don't address me as a guest" I started to make up my bed real quick as he just left after telling me to be quick and come downstairs for breakfast.

I had to take a shower so I had to rush things.

I entered the new bathroom, and damn, it was luxurious. It had a bath tub.

A freaking bath tub.

The shampoos smelled so nice and they also had my favorite sort of conditioner. God why does it feel so embarrassing to use these? It's just too out of blue. I was super pleased to see the sink, it was so freaking gorgeous. I wish I live here forever.

No not actually though.

I quickly took a shower, picked my outfit of the day, and sprinted downstairs as I was literally starving.

"Pancakes!" I boomed. They had pancakes for breakfast, pancakes with my favorite syrup. It's actually been a while since I had pancakes to be honest. I just really don't care because I'm starving.

Blair said "Take a seat Sage, I'll make us some coffee too, Trevor, do you mind bringing me some milk from the fridge."

Trevor was standing next to the fridge, busy with his phone. He didn't even bother to look up to Blair and just walked up to the table and sat down. Blair looked so done with him.

Brothers.

In a couple of minutes, we got our coffees, and finally some time to have a pleasant conversation. "Sage, you still have that bracelet on" Blair pointed towards the bracelet on my wrist. It was the silver, bulky bracelet, simple with no designs, that I wore everyday.

Every. Single. Day.

I never took it off. Because I just can't. It's impossible. Every attempt to cut it off or pull it out has been unsuccessful. I don't even remember when I wore this. My mother has told me that I can't take it off. I have legit no clue of what this thing is.

"Yeah, I still have it, I don't know why do I even have this thing on, I kinda wanna get rid of it" I exclaimed. Sometimes it's so annoying when people point out that I still have the bracelet on, like it's my wrist, why is it disturbing you. I'm already used to this thing now.

There was silence in the room, with just the annoying sound of Trevor chewing his pancakes. *Awkward.* I decided to break the silence by starting some chit chats "Blair I can't believe you actually started your own restaurant, I remember when you used to tell me that it was your dream to do so"

Does it ever drive you crazy, just how fast the night changes?

"Yes, I know right, its just makes me so happy that I can now proudly say that I accomplished my goal lets just hope that it grows well" said Blair, taking the dishes to wash them. Now she's gonna wash the dishes? Damn, she's so organized.

She's literally my favorite cousin, because she has her life all put up together. She's that one hallway crush of everyone. She doesn't speak too much, but she leads the most interesting conversations. She always has her coffee and books, and music. She has her style. There's something so deep in her eyes. That's why everybody stares at her. She has a beautiful soul. She is an art and not afraid to be different.

And then there's Trevor. I find him, *Selfish*. He is very organized too but, he is so cold. Though he looks really attractive, he has a confusing personality. He really is goofy and has the best jokes. My favorite thing about him is his freckles. You know what they say; *freckles are dust strewn across the face from heaven.*

Trevor and I headed towards their car so we could drive to work. I really wanted to see Houston better. I never would have guessed it such a beautiful city. I soon wanna visit more places in Texas but first I have to focus on my work and help Blair. I don't even know what I'm supposed to do with my life.

I'm lame.

Blair had the front seat, I was at the back and Trevor was driving. The place was 10 minutes away. I put my earphones on, and of course, Taylor swift!

My phone was about to die.

I forgot to charge it last night. I'm so screwed. I have to wait till we reach the place so I could charge it. So I just took out my book and began to read it. Yes, I read.

I was almost addicted to this book because I was so in love with the characters. I wish they weren't fictional, I mean, almost all the readers can relate.

The weather was hot; I mean its Texas so, Duh! I was wearing a simple white t-shirt with straight-leg jeans, and Blair was in a black tank top with shorts. Trevor was in his sky blue shirt and jeans. I swear I would kill myself if I forgot to keep my sunscreen with me.

I also wanted to visit a hair salon to get my hair a little change, I liked my brown hair but I needed some curtain bangs because why not. Although I wanted to cut my hair short with wispy bangs like Blair, who had dark black hair, I loved my super long hair. Trevor had black hair, which was always messy.

We were finally there so I kept my book back inside my bag, and got off. The restaurant was not so big in size but looked marvelous. It was white and black. There was a big sign on top. *Sunbread Woods*. The name of the restaurant.

I low-key disliked the name, not gonna lie.

There was a small pretty tree right outside. A leaf of the tree falls on Trevor's shoulder. "Trev, if a leaf falls on you, then a wish of yours will come true" said Blair with a warm smile. Trevor raised an eyebrow, then made a disgusted face and said "Yeah right, like I'm actually that stupid."

I mean it was obvious that it was a myth, my Mom also used to say this, but it's better than the weird tooth fairies and monsters under the bed.

This was such a Blair thing. She's just full of warmth and tenderness.

We moved inside and, holy biscuits, it was gorgeous. It felt so good to know that it's actually ours. The tables were beautiful, there were quotes hang on the wall, the wall was so pretty, I just couldn't wait to stand there on the counter.

We went in deeply to have a good look. There were many flower pots and plants around; the lights were just on point. We were literally so delighted, so much that Trevor had a smile on his face.

First I quickly charged my phone. After a while, some more people that we called arrived, I mean we obviously need waiters. "Sage, here," Blair handed me a bunch of aprons "You shall distribute it among the people" It looked so pretty, they had pink and black strips on it, with *Sunbread Woods* written on it. There wasn't a lot of advertisement of our restaurant but it was enough to attract customers.

"Trevor Woods! Oh my sweetheart, my dumpling it's been such a while, you've grown so much my child!" A random voice of an old lady appeared, I turned around to find an old lady, and she looked about sixty years old.

"Mrs. Adams, it's so good to see you here…OUCH" the lady pinched Trevor cheeks, as if he was a toddler. What's next? Did she buy candy for him or something? I could see how annoyed Trevor was.

"Who's she?" I whispered to Blair. "That's Trevor childhood teacher, she was actually also our neighbor and our mom's good friend, so you know" She said raising her shoulders.

The lady, namely Mrs. Adams, had a seat, she was looking around the place and she made a remark "This place reminds me of my childhood memories, you see, when I was your age……"

Not these boring stories again.

She really started reciting some boring stories of 'her time' and poor Trevor really had to listen to them. But wait, he was actually looking interested. I watched him listen really closely to his teacher.

"Trevor has a really close bond with Mrs. Adams, she was her all time favorite teacher and favorite aunt, and she always loved both of us as her own children" Blair said as she started to tie her apron.

Well it was obvious because I've never seen Trevor take interest in any old lady talks.

Moments later, different customers started to enter. And it finally looked like a real restaurant. And I really hope that our first day ends well.

Few years ago

I was on the ground, all dizzy; I could barely see the two other girls. They punched me, too hard.

Oh well I punched one of them first.

"How dare you hit me Sage, you've messed with the wrong person and you know what-" "Oh please Chloe, don't you think you deserved it?" I interrupted her, trying my best to stand up, before she kicks me back to fall.

Chloe and her minion Carrie, both are against me in this fight that I may or may not have made physical. I mean come on she really deserved it, after she talked crap about Amy.

"You're done, Sage, you're done" Chloe tried to push me back but I stopped her by grabbing her hands and trying to push her instead. Carrie, who's always a coward, just stood behind like a statue, I know she was unbothered but she tried to look worried or else she knew Chloe would kill her later anyway.

I pushed Chloe away as she gasped. I yelled at her "What is your problem Chloe, you know you can't beat me with heels on, plus you have your extensions, be careful Ms. Universe, you might go bald". She widens her eyes and hissed "At least I have the money to afford it loser, unlike you and that rat Amy". I rolled my eyes, fixed my hair and said "More like your daddy's money, princess, and if you dared to talk shit about Amy again, I'll keep punching you till you faint, or even better, die!" I didn't want her reaction, and I had no time to waste on her silly comebacks, so I just stormed off from there.

My body was aching so bad, specially my fist. It's not my first time punching someone to be honest. But it felt so good to punch Chloe. My arm hurts like hell because she literally tried to break it.

I had my classes, with Amy. Finally I could have some peace with people who actually care.

"Sage! Girl, I heard you got into a fight with Chloe, are you okay?" Amy held my shoulders and asked me, as soon as my closed my locker.

"Yes, I'm fine, and perhaps, isn't that a cool news, now I'll be more popular, because I punched Chloe in the face" I giggled. "This isn't funny Sage, you messed up, did you even thought about Mr. Ben?"

Oh my holy biscuits.

I totally messed up. Mr. Ben, my history teacher, is Chloe's dad. And if Chloe tells her dad about what I did to her, he will totally fail me in his class. Yes he is a jerk. He did that to a student, and no else teacher knew about how he failed a kid for no valid reasons. How did I not think of it while I literally punched her nose?

I'm like really bad at study, and I already failed a class. If I fail another class, they'll expel me.

"Oh no, what am I supposed to do!?" I gasped. Amy looked at me, I looked at Amy, she raised an eyebrow at me, and I raised an eyebrow at her.

Is she thinking what I'm thinking?

"Only *If*" we both said at the same time. "There's no chance at all that I'm actually apologizing to a brat like Chloe, but there might be a way to shut her running mouth" I said. She asked "Whatcha thinking?"

I seriously don't know myself.

I'm pretty sure we both thought that we'll actually murder Chloe. No that's a very bad idea! What the hell is wrong with me? I can't even bribe her; she's already a rich rascal. She's popular, she's rich, she's loved, and she's the queen of the school and the ruler of the Piano club- wait, piano club?

"Amy! Her piano club!" I jumped. "What piano club…….. OH her piano club! Yeah what about that" she says.

I turn around, my eyes searching for a person. I finally land on her. "You see her" I point at Emma, who's busy talking to her friends "That's Emma; she's also in the piano club with Chloe. You know how Chloe wants to be the first in everything, well except Math cause that's *nerdy* to her"

"Yeah she's too selfish, and?"

"Emma is better in the piano class than Chloe, and it will annoy her so much if Emma is praised by the school more than Chloe" Amy thinks about it "Oh, I see where you're going. It's actually an, Amazing idea! You're genius."

"I know right!"

"So how will we kidnap Chloe?"

Kidnap?

"What in the holy biscuits are you talking about" I ask her with full confusion. What the hell is she even thinking? "You're plan is to kidnap

Chloe and blackmail her telling that we will destroy her piano, that will help Emma rise, right?"

Gosh *Why*. Why is she so stupid? I stared at Amy for a while. Now I'm partially convinced that she's a psychopath.

"Are you kidding me? NO that's not what we're gonna do. And do you really think she can't afford another piano at the last minute?" Amy gives an awkward laugh.

"We're supposed to *help* Chloe, by ruining Emma's performance" Amy looks at me in shock "Sage! That's evil; Emma is like the sweetest kid ever in the entire school"

I know it's really cruel, but I have no choice. At least she'll score an A; I have to be evil to score at least a B. I still wish I didn't punch her on the nose. I always give myself anxiety attack.

"It's not like I hate her, but I don't want to fail, and perhaps, she'll never know" Why is school always so exhausting, I just wanna go home.

"Amy, do you wanna come over to my house, it's been so long" It's been months since Amy visited me, because of our busy schedules, high schools are stressing. "Yeah sure, I'm free today, so today at 4?" "Aight"

***

I was on my bed, with my legs straight up on the wall. I was reading a book. More like lost in it. I was obsessed with this book, I bought it yesterday and I'm almost done reading it. I had sleepless night yesterday reading 20 chapters. Insane isn't it? Sometimes I feel like books shouldn't cost money.

Believe me or not, I got addicted to books only last month and I completed four books. I have so many books in mind to read, I literally can't wait to finish one book and start reading another as fast as possible. But no worries, I'm gonna complete this book in no time, because it's not like I study or do chores.

I suddenly heard a knock on the door. I already knew it was Amy.

"Honey! Amy's here!" my mom called. I didn't move because I know she is coming upstairs to my room.

She enters the room, smiles at me, then looks at my book, then again looks at me but this time in disbelief.

"Since when did you start reading books?" She asks closing the door behind her and moving forward to sit down on a bean bag. "Eh, since a month or two, doesn't matter"

Last time she visited me, my room was boring and messy. But now it's organized, painted in pastel blue, has fairy lights, and has posters of Taylor swift, which sometimes makes me embarrassed when someone else notices it, it's too fan-girly. And then I have lots of pictures of me and Amy on a wall. She's like my only friend, my best friend.

My mom enters the room, super happy to see Amy after a long time. "Sweetie it's so nice to see, how's your mom doing?" Mom shouldn't ask this question, it's useless. Amy's mom is an arrogant, creepy and a grumpy woman. I remember when I visited Amy for the first time, when I was just six years old. She never smiled at me; she stared at me as if I was a murderer ready to kill her daughter. I felt hella uncomfortable around her and after that I SWORE I would never visit her, but I still have to because I don't want to make Amy feel bad.

I can't wait for Amy to move out, away from Ms. Darren, so called her Mom.

"She's amazing" Amy says, with a smile to my mom, definitely not for her own mom. *Fair enough.*

Amy's dad doesn't live with them, I know nothing about him, but I'm damn sure he's better than Ms. Darren.

"Amy, why don't you have dinner here tonight, I'm sure your mom wouldn't mind"

Oh yes she would. She's crazy.

"That's so sweet of you Mrs. Everitt, but I have things planned tonight" Amy says, scrunching her nose. Mom tells hers it's alright and she leaves.

We both actually had nothing special to do, so we decided to visit a nearby library to just hangout.

Libraries are the most interesting and satisfying places to ever exist. I mean, can you imagine, in a library, there are thousand of different books, and every book teaches us something different. Even though some books have the same color, some have same name, some has same size, and some even have the same author. But each book has a whole different world inside it. Some are filled with dragons; some are filled with beautiful heavenly fairies. Some of them tell about suicide, while some teaches about life. Some show us super toxic relationship, while some show beautiful love.

Is there any book which tells about a random silver bracelet stuck in your wrist for as long as you can remember?

Yeah, probably not.

Amy and I start picking random books, Amy is more into fantasy, and she loved Pegasus when she was young. Now she's obsessed with witchcrafts and witch land books.

While going through the teenage fiction section, my eyes spotted something odd. I found a really weird book, it's just weird. It's not weird because it's red in color, it's not weird because it's looks different from other books. It's weird because it has no name.

It doesn't have an author name. I decided to open it and read it, but failed because, the book is empty?

It is empty, like literally, all the pages are blank, it just has page numbers, and it had exactly 400 pages.

Why would someone keep such a random book in the library? Maybe it's someone's notebook, and they left it here by mistake. I open the first page, took out a pen from my pocket, and wrote a message for the person; by chance they come back looking for it.

'I hope you're doing great :)'

I don't know who that person is, but I'm sure this will make them smile. And it's a fact that, that person cannot be Chloe.

I placed the book back and went back to Amy. I found her sitting on the floor, reading a book, and two other books stacked beside her. This is her habit. Miss girl is living her main character moment.

I just realized I had to talk to her about something.

"Amy, we need to talk" I don't know why I sounded a little serious, as if she has done a crime and I'm here to arrest her. She looks up at me "Is something wrong?" she then gasps and stands up, and then asks "Don't tell me you knocked over the shelves, I knew it you're so dumb"

Jeez.

I mean, I *am* clumsy but is she serious right now?

"Amy! It's nothing like that. I wanted to talk to you about your birthday, it's in a week and you haven't planned anything about it."

Maybe she has already planned things, but hasn't told me. She usually plans her birthday a month ago, but she didn't this time. Maybe she forgot? Probably, because there is no reason to hide and lie.

"Oh yes I totally forgot to tell you that I planned a huge party this time and I've decided to invite many students from our school, this is going to be a blast because my mom is going out of town for a week just before the day of my birthday"

Okay that's a fortune. And by seeing her energy level and excitement telling me about the big party, I can tell this is going to be the best birthday party ever.

Sage

I am in a city, and it's not Houston. It's not in Texas or Ohio. It's a weird city, and I'm standing in the middle of a road. People seem fine to me.

Where is Blair?

Trevor?

Why in the holy biscuits am I alone in a city I don't even know? I started to ask people which place is this. But no one was stopping to answer me. They were walking past me and ignoring me, as if I was invisible.

Is this North Korea? But they don't look Asian. I finally made eye contact with a man, whose eyes were blue. Blue sparkling eyes, as if they are *filled with ocean.* His hair was brown, with a little bit of blond sprinkled on it. He looked different from other people around; he looked like he came straight from heaven. He was way more attractive than any other person around there.

We both stared at each other for longer than I thought, and now it felt awkward. He smiled at me, and he had dimples. I looked down, at my shoes, and then decided to approach him and ask him which place is this. I don't know why I felt nervous.

I walked towards him with a smile on my face, trying my best not to choke on my saliva "Hi, um, my name is-" "Sage?"

Wait, how does he know my name? Is he someone I know? Is he

Trevor's friend? But I don't even know where I am. But I'm sure it's not Texas.

"H…how do you k…know me?" I asked super confused. "Sage, I can't believe you're here" but then he stops smiling "Don't come up to me, please, don't hurt yourself"

What the heck?

Then suddenly I heard a weird and dizzy voice "Sage! Sage! Wake up you dumbo!"

I suddenly woke up in my bed. *It was another weird dream.* It was actually usual. I get really weird dreams, like REALLY weird.

Trevor was standing there, and I can see how annoyed he was. "Jeez, Trevor, you scared the crap out of me"

"Get your ass up and come downstairs for breakfast, I would not leave anything for you if you're not down in 20 minutes." He said to me and left.

I really need to get used to Trevor waking me up like that, because I always hit snooze on my alarm. Or maybe I just need to get myself to know that I'm employed now and need to get serious in order to earn money. Even though I know that my cousin is my boss, I need to be serious! I can't believe it's already been a week since our restaurant opened.

I sat on my bed with my feet on the floor. I picked up my phone and found that my mom had texted me. My dad already called me last night.

Mom: Hey sweetie, I hope you're doing great there in Texas. I know you wouldn't like it but, I already miss you :(

That sad face emoji makes it funnier. My dad already told me how much mom is missing me.

Me: Yes mom I'm great, and I miss you too. Right now I have to

head to work, I'll call you at 9 tonight.

I tossed my phone on my bed and rushed to the bathroom. I came downstairs after fifteen minutes to find Blair jumping in excitement and Trevor staring at the phone, as if he saw the best thing in the world.

I asked them what happened. "Sage! We just got a golden opportunity for our restaurant!" Blair beamed. She held my shoulder and said excitedly "A big influencer is going to visit our restaurant today, and after she's actually here, our restaurant will blow up!" seriously? An influencer? I mean, that's kind of lame to me but who cares? Today is going to be exciting!

All of us three couldn't wait to reach the restaurant, so we left as fast as we would. I even forgot to eat my breakfast, I'll just grab a star bucks later on.

We reach there, wear our aprons, I wore my cap, flip the open sign and guess what.

Just after ten minutes, our restaurant filled up with customers. There were literally so many people that we realized we needed to hire more people soon.

Our happiness was indescribable. Blair was so busy with managing things around. Trevor was administrating. I was at the counter taking orders, as well as delivery orders.

There were so much talking about that influencer, but no sign of her around.

I was just writing stuff down when another customer comes up to the counter "Hey there, is there a table for one" his voice was pleasant and attractive, it was kind of fruity. I looked up to meet blue eyes.

Blue eyes filled with ocean.

They were the same blue eyes, same brown hair. And the dimples, it were the same. I froze at the spot.

How is he a real person? I just stared at him as if I saw a ghost. I had lost all my senses. My heart was pounding. Not only because he was attractive as hell, but I doubted if he was real. I mean, I saw him in my dreams before I met him in real life. How is this even possible?

He waved his hand in front of my face and asked "Are you okay? Can I get a table for one, please?" it seem like he doesn't know me here, in my dream he knew my name, but he doesn't remember me now. Or maybe I'm just crazy.

I quickly came to my senses and said "Um, I…I am sorry, yes, please follow me" I took him to his table.

When he sat down, he kept glaring at me, with a smile on his face.

Gosh, he is a natural flirt.

I rushed back to the counter, and literally lost it. There were millions of questions rushing through my mind. *Who is he? How is he real? How was he in my dreams? How did he know my name then but not now?*

The big deal is that no one was there to answer these questions. I needed time to think about it so I just went the washroom.

More questions stormed in my mind. *Am I still* dreaming? *Have I gone crazy? Is he a hallucination? Have I lost my mind?*

I washed my face. Then suddenly I heard a person scream something. It didn't sound like a *help-me scream.*

I came out to find that the influencer just arrived. She also brought some of her friends. She had sunglasses on, a white crop top and white shorts. Her hair was tied in a pony-tail. And she had a black Dior bag, the one I've been wanting to buy for so long.

When she finally sat down, one by one people came to take pictures with her, others just clicked photos from their tables.

Like come on! She's not Taylor Swift.

She kind of looked haughty to me. I'm just spitting facts. When I was looking around, my eyes dropped at the blue-eyed guy (I don't know his name). He wasn't even looking at the influencer. He had headphones on. And he was busy with eating his lasagna.

I wasn't sure if he was aware that the influencer is here. And perhaps, I needed an excuse to talk to him anyway. I was about to go up to him, but wouldn't it be a little weird. I mean, first I lost my mind when I met him first, then I'm gonna go up to him randomly? What if he thinks I'm flirting with him?

I finally gathered all my courage to go up to him. I started walking towards him. But then I froze as he removed his headphones and looked around, his eyes met mine, my heart started to pound again. He smiled at me.

Gosh his dimples.

I got super nervous, I started to panic, so I turned around, took a long breathe, turned around again with a soft smile. I waved at him, as he waved back. I swear he might find me a weirdo. Gosh why do I have to embarrass myself like that?

I realized that he knew the influencer was here, but didn't care at all. That's totally understandable because I have the same case. That's a relief to me that I'm not the only one who doesn't know who this influencer is.

I didn't even realize that I was so busy being nervous that he almost finished. He ate the food like he hasn't ate anything for ages. He was about to leave. I really needed to talk to him and ask him if he knew me already or something like that. As soon as I wanted to run towards him, Trevor called "Sage! If you don't mind, can you stand at the counter, ma'am?" I understood his sarcasm very well. I tossed my arms in the air, as a gesture of annoyance, and then went back to the counter.

After a long day of work, all of us were exhausted. It was almost 9 and I had to call my mom. She would understand if I was late. We all cleaned up the place, Blair was looking through her phone, I think she found more employs. We had enough chefs, we needed waiters. Kind of ironic for me. We all sat down on the chairs. Blair also told us that our restaurant actually blew up on social media.

"Hey guys, tomorrow is my sister's wedding, remember?" said Noah, one of the workers of our restaurant. Tomorrow is his sister's wedding, and this might be a good opportunity to have a little fun. "Yes we remember, don't worry, we'll be there on time"

We all come towards our car and get ready to reach home. I sat in the back seat and took out my phone to call my mom. "Sage, who was that guy," asked Trevor. I looked up at him, a little shocked that he noticed me staring at that guy. I knew he was talking about the *Blue-eyed* guy. How am I supposed to tell them who he was? "Which guy?" asked Blair to both of us. Trevor started to drive and said "Our Sage was flirting with a customer"

"Wait really Sage? Oh my Gosh tell me the story" Blair had a wide smile on her face. "Trev, what in the holy biscuits are you talking about?"

"Oh so you think you're smart enough to play innocent. Come on, I saw how nervous you were with him. But Sage, it's a little weird" Trevor said. "What's weird?" I asked him. I swear I will choke him to death if he calls him a *ignoramus twerp*.

"I was unable to look at his face"

What does he mean? The guy literally kept his head up and smiled at everyone he passed by. Trevor needs glasses, I already told Blair.

I didn't ask Trevor anything because I knew he's crazy and I don't want to talk about him anymore. Trevor takes a turn to a store "We need eggs" he says this and gets out of the car to buy them.

Blair turns to me and asks excitedly "So who exactly is this lucky guy?" I looked at her and leave a big sigh. "Blair, I swear it's nothing, I just thought I already knew him, it was a misunderstanding."

Blair's smile fades away. Now she had concern in her eyes. "Is there something you're hiding?" Wow, she doesn't even study psychology but reads me so good. I look down at my phone, trying my best to avoid eye contact. "No" I said, with so much straight-forwardness. I usually speak a lot so just saying a simple *No* was weird to me. It was a little awkward too. Blair stares at me for a few seconds, then turns around. I called my mom and I was a little surprised how quickly she picked up. I placed it on speaker because I was checking if the house keys are still with me in the purse or not.

"Sage! My baby how are you? It's been so long since I heard your voice" Mom says this so loudly that it made Blair giggle. "Yes Mom I'm doing great and I missed your voice too"

"I have some great news for you"

"Let me guess, it's related to Evelyn" I already guessed it because my mom loves talking about my sister more than me. Evelyn and I were never close because when I was in high school, she lived with our aunt, because, I don't know. It's so ironic isn't it? She still visited us on holidays and weekends. But, whenever I asked mom why can't Lyn live with us, like a normal family, she would usually evade the question.

"Yes, she got accepted into Stanford! Can you believe it? Other mom's are going to be so jealous!"

Blair looks at me, amazed, I can tell she' congratulating me for my sister. "Wow, I'm so happy for her, give her a hug from me" then I started to feel a little down, so I asked "Mom? Are you disappointed in me?"

"What? No honey, absolutely not, I'm proud of you both, and I love you"

A smile takes place on my face; Blair looks at me with a pout. I can tell she wants to say that my mom is so cute.

"Thanks mom, I love you too" Then suddenly I heard dad scream on the phone, with other men. "Is everything okay there?"

"Oh yes honey, your dad and his friends are watching sports, and I don't know which one is it"

Probably football. Then mom says something that completely ruined my mood.

"Sage, I just wanted to tell that Amy…." "I don't care mom" I said immediately. I didn't want to hear her name. So I just told my mom bye, and hung up.

I sat straight with my arms crossed, I was looking out of the window. I wanted to have a blank mind at that time, I didn't wanted to think of anything. I wanted to avoid the feeling of this pain. But that's the thing about it, the pain, it demands to be felt.

Blair looked at how overwhelmed I was. "It's okay Sage, I know you're trying to forget everything, but at the positive side, whatever happened to you in your past just made you stronger-"

I interrupt her "I didn't need to be stronger, I was a child, a teenager of about fifteen-sixteen, I needed to be safe, not strong" I didn't wanted to cry but tears started to form in my eyes. I tried to change the subject "What the heck is Trevor doing for long, did he kill himself"

Just as I said that, Trevor opens the car gate and sits. "I'm so sorry I made ya'll wait, something crazy happened inside" Then suddenly the shopkeeper comes outside and shouts "Never come back here" Trevor yells back "Shut up man!"

Blair and I both looked at each other. Trevor closes the car window and starts the car as he speaks "When I bought the eggs, a crazy drunk man pushed me from behind and I dropped the eggs, and it broke, then I lost my mind and punched the man in the face" Blair brought her hands to her forehead, and we both understood where it was going.

"Then the shopkeeper started yelling at me, and I again lost my mind and tried to punch the shopkeeper but some other men stopped me, then I had pay for the violence created and the broken eggs" Me and Blair were literally speechless. I knew he was crazy but I didn't know he was *this* crazy.

"But don't worry ladies, I got the eggs" He said that with a childish giggle, which made both of us laugh.

Few years ago

"Chloe listen to me!" I kept running after Chloe, Amy behind me.

"Listen loser, I will not accept your apology, wait till my daddy hears what you've done"

I frown throwing my head back. "Chloe at least listen to what I'm trying to tell you"

Amy taps my shoulder and whispers to me "Not here" Yeah she has a point; I don't want anyone to hear our plan and inform Emma about it. I nod, then grab Chloe's wrist and pull her to the washroom. "What the hell do you think you're doing?"

"Listen, I know it might sound weird, but please don't tell your dad-" Chloe laughs like witch and then shouts "Oh yes I will!" she tries to walk away.

Amy pulls her shoulder "Shut up Chloe and listen to what we're trying to tell you, can't you just shut your damn mouth for a second or two. For God sake, if you'd run like you tongue, you'd be in a better shape, all you do is babble useless things, why do you have ears? Just for your expensive ear rings and piercings? Why don't you put them to work and freaking listen to us!!!?"

I and Chloe widen our eyes as Amy flames up. "Jeez, chill. Alright girls, what do ya'll wanna talk about" Chloe casually leans towards a door, looking at her new nails, *Fake nails.* I hate it when she's so sassy.

"Look, let's make a deal okay?" I tell her, making hand gestures, as she raises an eyebrow and gestures her hand as to *what deal.* Amy casually walking to and fro with her arms crossed, also checking if someone's hearing us or not.

"I will help you score better in your piano club, and in return, you forget that I punched you" Chloe again laughs. I want to punch her again so bad. Amy and I look at each other. I know she wants to punch her too.

"You? *You* help me score better?" She laughs again. Her laugh is the most annoying thing in the world now. It was kind of awkward just watching her laugh so I thought to piss her off.

"Yes, me, because you already know Emma is way better than you" I said, standing like a queen, with my arms crossed, chin up, and staring deep in Chloe's eyes. Amy stood behind with a smirk, rolling her eyes. "You know, your daddy won't like it really much if you come second position in your club, how pathetic." Holy biscuits, I felt more powerful than Chloe. I looked back at Amy with my head tilted a little bit, and I know we both want to laugh like an idiot at the moment.

When I look back at Chloe, my smile kind of drops. Chloe was looking down, and she was..........*terrified?* Never in my life had I imagined this scenario. I can feel Amy being uncomfortable. Because it's usually Chloe who bullies us. *Are we bullying Chloe?*

"It's not my fault Emma is better, she has *interest* in piano." Chloe says anxiously. Does that mean Chloe doesn't like piano?

"I don't like piano, and I don't like the other clubs I've joined and came first in, like my art club, or drama" she's literally tearing up, *what am I supposed to do now*. Oh my gosh, this is the perfect time to manipulate Chloe, I know it's wrong but eh.

"You guys assume that my dad buys all of the stuff I want, he treats me like a princess and stuff like that, but the truth is that he just wants me to look rich to maintain our family's class and standards, he doesn't care about me. He also pressures me to come first in everything so he can brag about me to the other teachers, and it kind of becomes easy for me because I don't have friends for distraction"

The atmosphere was becoming blue and gloomy. Amy asks "What do you mean you don't have friends, you're literally the most popular girl of the school, and you have tons of friends."

Chloe glares at Amy, then her tears actually start dropping, she cried "I don't have friends; they're all fake, why would anyone befriend a brat like me? They all just want my riches, and want to be popular by being my friend, or they just want to brag about being close to a *teacher's kid*. You know nothing, ya'll just judge me"

Wow, that hit me like a train. I never expected to hear so much from her. It's usually really hard to say what's going in Chloe's mind because she's either being sassy, or angry. I bet this is the first time seeing Chloe in so many emotions. I never would have guessed she goes through so much. Is it weird that I feel sorry to punch her?

"I am just a *human*, I feel pain, I trip and fall, I cry, I talk to myself because only I know what I go through. I am just a human, I get puzzled, I mess up, I feel devastated, voices in my head humiliate me" Chloe wipes away her tears.

I and Amy were frozen at the spot. This all happened so fast, it's gonna take some time process. Chloe was about to walk out, but she stops and asks "And what did you mean by you can help?"

I blink three times, give out a big sigh, then try to talk about our plan, but it's hard to talk when your mind is still processing about what just happened. I look back at Amy, she nods, telling me to tell her.

"Yea, well, um, we can help you come first in your piano club, by, ah, ruining Emma's performance" I say, squinting my eyes.

This kind of feels weird and bad to say. Chloe raises her eyebrows, and her face glow up. "Really? You think you can do that. Oh hell yea! Let's do it" Wow, her duality is insane"

"Are ya'll sure you won't mess up? Because I don't trust you losers at all"

Is she the same Chloe who was crying to us a few minutes ago? No wonder people call her two-faced. "You can trust us Chloe, but remember the deal, forget that I punched you"

She smirks at me "Which punch? I already forgot about it" she winks at me and leaves.

I and Amy look at each other with wide smiles. We started to jump and laugh with excitement "Sage we did it!" "I know right, we manipulated her so easily!"

Amy stops jumping and looks at me with a little disappointment and says "Hey, Do you think what we're doing is right? Because, we're doing it unfair with Emma. You punched Chloe, but Emma has to suffer." Well, I guess I never thought about it that way. But I don't have a choice. It's too late to think about it now. I never thought I could be so evil.

"It is what it is, but thank you for being so thoughtful"

Sage

My eyes were closed, and I know it's time to wake up. I'm thinking about how we will spend the whole day at the wedding. I don't want to wake up yet, so I'm waiting for my *human-alarm* named Trevor.

It's been 20 minutes since I snoozed my alarm, but Trevor didn't come to wake me up. I don't hear anyone. Am I dreaming again?

I slowly open my eyes, just to find Trevor sitting on the floor in front of me and staring me intensely. I scream and sit on my bed alarmed because he looks like an expressionless ghost. He scared the shit out of me. I exploded at him "Bro what the heck are you doing here and why are you staring at me, you scared me as freak"

"Sage, help me" he said, coming towards me by crawling with his knees and folding his hands together. "What happened?" I asked him, totally confused what the hell is going on in this house.

"I messed up, very bad" he trembled. He was about to tell me what happened but got interrupted by a noise.

"TREVOR!!" Blair screamed at the top of her lungs. Then she dashes into my room, with a…………..*broom*? She started chasing Trevor "I'M GONNA HIT YOU SO HARD THAT YOU'LL PASS OUT!!"

They looked like Tom and Jerry. I hold Blair by her waist and stop her from running. She started crying like a baby "SAGE!!" she was sobbing

"THIS TREVOR RUINED MY FAVOURITE WHITE DRESS! WHAT WILL I WEAR TO THE WEDDING?!"

Now things started to make sense. I look at Trevor; he was passed out on the floor after running for his life. I never knew he was such a trouble maker. "Trev, what did you do?"

He looks up at me, sits down and states "Well, I may or may not have poured a few drops of my coffee on her dress" Blair drops a death glare on Trevor and again yells "I WILL BITE YOU!"

"OKAY! I accidently poured a whole cup of my coffee on her dress, but come on, it could have been worse" he says, again passing out on the floor, breathing soundly.

Now that Blair's dress has an extreme coffee stain, it is wasted and cannot be fixed. *Thanks a lot, Trevor.* I pat Blair's back "Don't worry about it, I have an extra dress, well, I stole it from Evelyn, but you can wear it today" She looks at me with her eyes widen "Really? Oh my god Sage you're such a life saver! Thank you" She hugs me then stands up to leave, she kicks Trevor. "Ouch"

When both of them went outside, I felt a little pain on my right wrist. It was the bracelet. My hand was all red. It happened usually and I was used to it. I remember how Amy always tried to break it with a rock because I told her how bad it hurts sometimes. She always failed. Once I even got a scratch on my wrist because she tried to pull it out. She also almost punched a random boy because he made fun of me calling me a *'bracelet-dimwit'*

I quickly took a bath, change into my clothes and went into Blair's room to get our makeup done. Trevor already got ready. He was just wearing a common black suit. Sometimes I wish things for us women were as easy as they are for men. He barely took thirty minutes to get ready, whereas we're gonna take two hours to do our makeup and hair. Trevor enters the room with another cup of coffee in his hand. "How long are ya'll gonna take?" he says, sipping his coffee. He's totally a coffee addict.

"Keep that cup of shit away from us" Blair said glaring at Trev. "Eh" then he leaves.

We finally got ready. Blair had her short hair straighten. I did a blowout for my hair. We had light yet drop-dead gorgeous makeup. We both had a white fit and flare dresses.

Trevor was waiting in the car. I swear it was hard walking with heels after a long time.

We got at the place just in time and holy biscuits, it looked stunning. I literally want to run inside like a kid. We met Noah shortly after we entered the place.

Blair and I just wanted to meet the bride. We went to have a look at her, she was just chilling. I mean obviously because we're hours early. But she looked so tired. We sat there for a while and had some chit chatting. But then, I smelled something. *Food.*

I told Blair I'm going outside, and then left.

There were tons of snacks on the tables. Chocolates! The kids were just grabbing the snacks and running away. I don't think anyone would notice if I picked one, or maybe two.

I started looking around, pretending to admire the decors, slowly walking towards the table. I don't really care if I get embarrassed. Or maybe I do. I just want to eat something! I didn't do my breakfast quite well. As soon as my hands were about to grab a chocolate, someone calls my name from behind. I flinch and turn around quickly. I had an awkward smile on me. It was Noah.

"Hey what are you up to?" he asks while raising his eyebrows. I don't think he noticed anything. I finally rest my face and smile *normally* then said "Oh nothing, just wondering around you know. But Noah, the decors are amazing, and your sister looks dazzling." He gives a wide smile and keeps his hand on his heart "Well, my sister is only gonna get married once so I guess it's worth it. Hey, why don't you get some snacks" Wait really; he said I could get some snacks! "The coffees and biscuits are over there" he was pointing to the other side of the large table. Of course he was talking about the boring snacks, but I wanted chocolate. I smile and nod, pretending to leave. As soon as Noah turns around, I grab a chocolate and ran away.

Trevor was drinking another cup of coffee. "Third cup? Seriously?"

"Eh I don't care"

Then I notice a chocolate in his hand. Thank god I'm not the only one stealing chocolates. "Where's Blair?" he asked me, biting into his chocolate. "Somewhere away from these cups filled with coffee" He rolls his eyes.

"Trevor! Sweetie, look we met again" That's the old lady again. The Teacher lady. What in the world is she doing here? The world is so small. "Oh, Mrs. Adams, what a coincidence" said Trevor, smiling at her. I just wanted avoid them so I walked away, looking for Blair.

There were so many different drinks to try. I almost drank a lot that I might throw up.

I took a seat because my feet were paining because of the heels. And I just realized that I haven't met the groom yet. Ugh, where is Blair? I want to visit him with her.

I look around, but still unable to find Blair. I saw Trevor, busy with the other random guys; I see he got rid of Mrs. Adams.

I saw a person standing alone, just busy with the snacks and drinks. And he was also eating a chocolate. I already knew every grown up is stealing chocolates here. When he turns around, I meet blue eyes.

Blue eyes filled with ocean.

And once again my soul left my body. Is he following me? Nah that doesn't make sense. This is probably a big coincidence. But the dream wasn't a coincidence. What in the holy biscuits is happening?

He notices me right away. He again smiles his *dimply smile* at me. I don't even know if *dimply smile* is a thing but eh. Why does he always smile at me? He probably recognized me because we met at the restaurant. But this time I swear I'm gonna talk to him about what is going on with me.

I don't smile back, I just walk up to him because I somehow gained superhuman strength. I am so freaking nervous but I have to do it. "Hey" I say to him. He widens his eyes, looks around then points himself, as to confirm if I'm talking to him. I nod. But then I'm unable to say anything, I just stare at him.

"Are you……aren't you a worker at the Sunbread Woods?" I knew he recognized me. I think I should not get weird and start off a casual conversation.

I smile a soft and pretty smile at him "Yes, Hi, I'm Sage Everitt" I bring my hand forward to offer a handshake. I don't know why but I felt like I could read him, his face, and his blue oceanic eyes. They said he wants to continue this conversation.

"Nice to meet you again, Sage" he shakes my hand and kept the eye contact.

I don't know how to start a conversation between us, but I really hated this awkward silence. I grab two drinks from the table and offer him one glass. "Follow me" I said as I started to walk away to a place where there are fewer people. I really don't want Trevor to find me talking to him again. He follows me. I think he is all by himself here.

We reach a lower balcony, with a beach view. He started to laugh. His laugh is so contagious and wholehearted. I started to laugh too. I don't know why we're laughing. "You're so enthusiastic" he said. Wow, am I? Nobody told me this before. "So, do you want to talk to me about something? Because I saw you wanted to approach me yesterday too." He asked me, squinting his eyes, and looking down at me. He is visibly taller than me. I'm surprised how he didn't ask if we've met before or not.

"Well, yeah, but it doesn't really matter" I lied because I feel like I will be looking creepy to him if I ask some weird questions to the poor guy. He chuckles. *Ugh, his dimples.*

I realized that I still call him the blue-eyed guy. "Hey, what's your name?" I ask him. He turns his gaze away from me, looking at the beach. He looked like he was thinking. Why was he thinking about his name though?

"I don't have a name"

What.

"You don't have a *name*? How come? So are you like, Nameless?" Well I guess everyone calls him *ocean eyes*.

He laughed "Yeah I guess. I mean, I don't have anyone in my family, or any friend to talk to. I'm still looking for job. When I have literally no one to talk to, I guess I don't have a name?"

Interesting.

That sounds like a lie. That is weird but I don't know why I don't find it weird. I stare at him for a while, still processing the thing he just told me. Is he lying?

He smiles, seeing me confused. "Long story short, I wake up alone, live alone, and sleep alone. I don't know for how long this has been going." That's sad. I feel bad for him. "Your parents?"

"I'm an orphan, for as long as I can remember" His face says he doesn't want to talk about it, so I don't say anything next.

"Well you need to get a name, because now you have a friend" I smile. He looks at me, a little amazed. "I'll call you Clyder" This name just popped up in my head. I don't know why, but it does sound attractive.

"Clyder, I like that" He looked so glad.

He likes it, of course he does.

Then he started to think about something really hard. He was zoned out. So I decided to tell him more about me.

"Sunbread Woods belongs to my cousin, and I help her there. I came to Houston a month ago. I lived in Ohio."

"Wow, you're interesting. And Ohio, it's nostalgic" he says while dimples form on his cheeks again. Maybe he has been to Ohio before; I don't know what's so nostalgic there. For me it was a disaster.

Talking to him felt like we've been friends forever, he's way more fun, interesting and comforting than Amy. I know there shouldn't be comparison between them but it's the first thing that came to my mind.

"So from what relation are you here? Since you don't have a family" he fixes his hair back, smiles at the sky, then says "It's a secret but, I actually sneaked in" I almost chocked on nothing at that point. He sneaked in my friend's wedding and I'm enjoying talking to him? "I just sneaked in for food, because I need it, I always do that. I do have money to buy stuff but, it's just funny, you know."

Wow, he's a thief. I wonder why he told me this big secret. It doesn't feel wrong though. I'm sorry for his life. He looks at me and says "You're gonna throw me out aren't you?" I laugh at his face "Well, I am supposed to do that, but I won't. Just don't eat everything up" He chuckles on that joke.

We kept talking about our interests, past, and so much more, until I heard Blair.

"Sage! Where are you! The ceremony is about to start" and I panicked.

"Clyder! I need to go, until I see you again, pretend you don't know me" I told him that because I don't want to answer Trev's questions and turned around to leave when he said "It's impossible to forget today, and you. Lets meet again, Sage, I want to learn so much about you" He smiled and waved a bye to me, so did I.

All through the ceremony, I tried not to think about Clyder. I saw him dig in the food, a lot. I didn't want to embarrass him, so I tried to ignore him.

The day ended, so did the wedding. We were really tired and it was really late now. So we decided to go home. We had to pick up McDonalds for dinner.

Trev starts driving and Blair asked me "Sage, where were you the whole time?"

"She was stealing chocolates" Trevor says, really innocently.

"Ah! Only me? What about your coffees?" I flare my nostrils at him, raising my chin. "Do not question me, coffee is a necessity. I can't even-"

"TREV TURN! MCDONALDS!!" Blair interrupted him, when he almost forgot to turn to McDonalds.

"Oops" I knew he couldn't do anything right.

While Trev was ordering food from the drive-thru, I put my air pods on and look out the window. I was again thinking about Clyder.

I'm still curious about why he told me his secret, I just met him.

Few years ago

"Amy, chill. Stop panicking, I'll be there" I put the call on speaker as I do my hair. It's been about a week since we talked to Chloe. Luckily, she didn't tell her dad anything.

"I don't know, I just don't have a good feeling about it. Do you think we can stop this, we might plan something else?"

"Oh my god, Amy. Are you on *my* side or Emma's? You constantly doubt me. It's like you want me to fail. Remember, if I fail, I'll get expelled. Don't give me and chance to blame you for this"

She pauses for a few seconds, then sighs "Look, don't get me wrong, Sage. I just don't want us to get in trouble"

"I'll reach school in about half-n-hour, remember to reach back-stage on the second bell, I hope you're not mad"

"No, it's alright" then she hangs up.

Today is the day. I really don't want to disappoint Chloe. We're gonna break some keys of her piano, at the very last moment. And if that won't be enough, we're gonna ruin the performance by messing up the lights, speaker, or maybe distract her by something so she messes up. Just one mistake on stage will be enough to help Chloe score well than Emma.

I was digging in my breakfast. "Honey, guess what" my dad says, as he sat down to take breakfast on the table with us. "What dad?" he smiles and says "Lyn is coming over today!" Ugh, Evelyn. "Wow, how sweet, have fun" I couldn't think of anything but sarcasm.

"Sweetie, she's your sister, please" Mom says as she serves dad his food. I still don't understand why I have to accept her? First she left our family to live with our aunt, and there wasn't even a valid reason. And she visits us whenever she wants. She's a spoiled brat. But still, all mom and dad do is talk about her. Sometimes they make me feel unappreciated.

"Thanks for the food" I leave my chair and just stomp out of the house, grabbing my bag. After I leave the house, I pause and wondered if I was too rude with them.

Just forget it.

My mind is too occupied today; I can't waste my time on thinking about Evelyn. I wait at the bus stop, when I saw Ms. Darren and Amy walk over here. Looks like Amy missed her bus, so she's taking mine. But why is her mom here?

"Good morning Ms. Darren, what brings you here?" I throw a fake smile at her, knowing she won't smile back. First she takes a look on my outfit, which was a little too inappropriate for her, BUT IT WAS OKAY! She's a Karen.

"I had some work, Amy, just because you're with her right now, doesn't mean you get to bunk school today" her voice and tone was so sassy. She rolls her eyes at me, then leaves.

What in the holy biscuits is wrong with this woman? I swear, soon she'll call me a criminal. I look at Amy with a *what-the-hell* look. She raises her shoulders as she can't do anything.

The bus arrives shortly after her mom left. We both sit together, and didn't say a word to each other for a while. The students at the back were making hella noise. The weather outside was opposite. It was pleasant and quite. It looked so aesthetic.

"I'm sorry" Amy states and then I look at her "I'm sorry for doubting you, and also for my mom. I am such a coward, right?"

I smile, then take her hands in mine "Absolutely not, you're strong, really brave, and I know for a fact that you just want the best for me" She smiles and looks down, fidgeting with her fingers.

That's why I love her so much, she knows how to fix things. She's probably the only person after my parents to love me so much. Sometimes I fear that I might lose her, but that never happened in the past several years. And I heard that people who are together for more than seven years are meant to be together.

Then we both look out the window. I wish she's thinking the same thing I am. I wish she's looking at me right now. But you know what, it doesn't matter if she's looking at me or not, because we're looking at the same sky together, which is better than anything. Anybody can look at you, but it's rare to find someone who looks at the world the same way as you do.

"Sage," she says, still looking outside "You might be the best person of my life, the only one who understands me" I don't know if I'm imagining stuff or what, but I see her brown eyes sparkling like the moon, but is covered with honey from heaven.

I want to tell her the same too, she's way better than Evelyn. I told her "Remember when I told you that I talk to the moon at night?" She laughs and nods.

"The moon tells me about the Sun, and I tell him about you" she gives a very warm smile "Oh my god, so cheesy". We both turn away and continue to admire the nature, even though I want to admire her more.

We finally arrive at school. We had different classes first. We would have to bunk our second class to get to backstage.

As I enter the class, I bump into Emma and knock her books down. "I'm so sorry!" Yes Emma, I'm so sorry, for what I did right now, and what I'm about to do soon. "Oh its okay, I'll pick it up, don't worry about it" then she smiles.

Gosh, why does she have to be so sweet?

I feel so guilty. When I look up, I find Chloe glaring at me, she was chewing gum, and was surrounded by her minions. I try my best to avoid any contact with her, and sit away from her.

The whole class I was just tapping my pen, full of anxiety. I am about to do something very wrong. It might not be a big deal for other people like Chloe, but me and Amy don't get involved in school dramas. We are about to bunk class to mess with someone's academic life.

My life is a disaster.

The bell rang. I look at Chloe and she looks at me. Without a second thought, we both grab our bag and rush to the auditorium. I can hear some girls yell Chloe's name. And why won't they, their Miss Queen is running away without a notice.

How cringe.

I suddenly stop at Mr. Smith's class, waiting for Amy to come out fast. As soon as I saw Mr. Smith leave, I scream "Amy come on, we don't wanna mess up the last minute!" Everyone started staring at me and I could here them gossip "What a weirdo" but I really don't care. Amy came out and I realized, Chloe already headed to the auditorium. Ugh.

When we reached there, we noticed that Emma had the first performance. Shit. Now we had to do things right. Chloe is in front of the stage, she cannot go back stage. Emma is rehearsing on the stage.

We go backstage, just waiting for the right moment. "Listen Amy, first you have to break the keys, break the frequently used ones"

"Are you stupid? How do I know which ones are frequently used? I don't play a piano!" Oh yeah, right. Anyways.

We just keep quite and keep an eye on the stage from side. Then we saw Emma leave to use the bathroom.

That's the chance.

"Amy go go go!" I gesture her to go. She quickly runs to the stage and hides behind the giant piano. My heart is beating so fast. I've never done such a mischief before. I could see the fear on Amy's face as she carefully takes out few keys.

Then I suddenly saw her flinch and hide again. She looks at me with a terrifying look and signs me something.

That sign meant that we're dead.

She's gonna get caught, Oh no! This can't be happening! We can't get caught. I feel so terrible to drag Amy into this.

Then I look at Amy, she runs down to me. She's breathing heavily. We don't say anything, but just get to the backstage.

"I'm so sorry Amy! Believe me, I never wanted to drag you into this" I tremble. She calms down and looks at me "It's okay, we didn't got caught," Thank god! "We almost did but I ran away. Emma's gonna perform in about five minutes"

This is so stressful. I regret punching Chloe so much. But it really doesn't matter now. Past is past. We cannot change it.

We wait for five minutes, just fidgeting, and then suddenly we heard the teacher say "Okay Emma lets watch you perform first"

PANICK. We both run towards the stairs and reach the space above the stage. As soon as Emma sat down to play, many teachers sat down too. The lights went deem and the spotlight was on Emma.

I saw Emma worrying when she saw her missing keys. But she can't do anything because, the show must go on. She knew she messed up, but she continued to perform. Now time to cause some chaos.

I turn the spotlight the other way. But Emma didn't stop, and wait, how is she playing so well? She's supposed to lose notes.

The lights turn on again. Dang it! I point Amy to do what I told her to. She nods. She then takes an elastic rubber band and places it between her two fingers then points at Emma's face. She takes small bits of paper that are big enough to hit her face hard.

She aims, and shoots, and kept shooting till she messes up. But she kept tolerating and didn't mess up once.

Why is Emma so freaking good at this?!

I was loosing my temper. "Just mess up you bonehead!" I mumbled to myself. Amy looks at me and whispers "What now?"

I look around in hope to find something to help. I found a bottle of water. There is no way this won't work. Our last hope.

Without wasting a second, I pour the whole bottle on her, Amy gasped at that sudden movement. But I could still hear Emma play. I look down to find that the water was too little and it poured more on the piano than Emma. She wasn't affected and kept slaying.

I lost my mind at that time. I am having some serious anger issues right now. I wanted to throw fire at her.

EMMA, MESS UP ALREADY!

I saw a big light system, which was big enough to break the piano, *or even Emma's head.* I start to open the screws so it falls down. I was being too aggressive. There is only one thing going on my head at that time.

I don't wanna fail.

I don't wanna get expelled.

I can't let this happened.

I opened one screw, and then Amy realized what I was doing. She widens her eyes and started to pull me away and take my downstairs. I pushed her once but she didn't stop "Sage, have you lost it? Do you even realize what you're doing?"

"I don't care! Go away and let me do what I'm doing!" I yell at her. Amy successfully drags me downstairs, even though I was pushing her so hard. Now I want to punch Amy.

"You're trying to kill her! What has gotten into you?!" She says holding my shoulders. I pause.

Oh my god. What was I about to do? I bring my palms to my face. I can't believe that I almost crossed the line. I was about to hurt Emma. I'm a Maniac.

I remove my hands and revealed my teary face to Amy. She hugs me. I could hear everyone clap for Emma's excellent performance.

I was……..crying. Crying because I tried to injure someone, crying because I failed on my task, crying because I'm gonna get expelled and leave Amy.

Amy pats my back "its okay, Sage, it's alright, we tried our best" I sob "No it's not, I almost became a monster and I would never forgive myself for this. I'm so sorry" She pushes me back from the hug and holds my shoulders again "No, you don't have to apologize for this, because no one apologized for making you this monster"

"No! I shouldn't have punched Chloe, and definitely not have planned to do shit to Emma, and shouldn't have think of hurting her, I deserve this"

"So, you believe you made a mistake?" I look at her and nod. She smiles and says "Then that's it, you realized you were wrong and that's more than enough. You know, it's never too late to do the right thing, but good for you, you didn't mess up anything, so you're okay"

My heart feels so light and my mind feels relieved. I don't even know what I did to deserve her. I hug her again but this time, tighter. I want to say thank you, but I know that if I say anything, I will break in tears.

Suddenly someone came from behind, grabs my arm and turns me around. Than she held my collar and glared at me.

It was Chloe.

Amy screamed "What the heck Chloe?!" "Shut up you pillock!" she yells back at Amy, then glares back at me. Her eyes are dark and cold. Her voice tone was deep and she was sweating in anger. "You messed up Sage, I CAME SECOND, AGAIN. You said I could trust you? You gave me your goddamn word!" She was breathing noisily. She doesn't scare me but whatever she could do, scares the freak out of me.

Amy tries to pull me and away from her, but her grip is strong. I am physically strong enough to push her and punch her again. But I felt like my body isn't functioning. So much happened in the past twenty minutes. She was saying more stuff but I couldn't hear them, I was overwhelmed.

I push her very hard, then runaway from the spot. I ran to the bathroom. Then I froze for a few seconds. Sadness crushed me with the overwhelming force of a tidal wave and I drowned in its embrace. I wasn't crying, but angry. Actually, I don't care if I get expelled, I was scared for some other reason. If I drop out, my parents will shift me to another city, and I don't want to leave Columbus, I can never leave Amy.

I washed my face and looked in the mirror. I don't know how to react. I don't want to let Amy know that I'm going to leave, I just don't know how I'm going to start. I want to cry, but I felt like I don't have tears left. I don't want to think about anything right now.

I turned around to leave, when I saw Amy walk in. She looks at my red face for a few seconds before saying "Are you okay? I'll leave, if that's what you want" I nod aggressively and said "No, never leave me, please" She sighs and said "It's okay, we'll find another way to help you"

Yes, I want to find another way to help me. But, I don't want to do anything else that will get us in trouble. I want to make another plan and do something else to stop Chloe from informing her dad. But I feel so miserable that I just want to go home, lock my room and cry my heart out. I don't want to get expelled but I want to forget everything for a moment and relax. And the fact that I still have tons of classes left just leaves me exhausted.

***

After hours of classes, we finally get to run away from hell. "Will your mom be at home right now?" I ask Amy. "I don't really think so, she said she'll be late, and pretty sure she'll be back home after eight" I take out my phone to check the time and asked her "Wanna go to a café to complete homework"

We never really did that. Actually, I usually just forget my homework, I mean, who doesn't? It might be my first time to ask Amy to do homework with me. Amy is always really determined and motivated while studying, she believes that she can be a great lawyer. She wants to go to law school so impatiently and eagerly.

But homework isn't even the reason to go to café; the reason is, to avoid going to my house. I am not in the frame of mind to argue about Evelyn.

Sometimes I avoid calling my house 'home' because there is a difference. House is human made buildings, made up of bricks and cement, where a family lives. But a home is a place, or a feeling of comfort and love, where we don't have to lie about how we feel, because we know that the people of our home are understanding.

Amy finds my question ironic and says "Yeah I mean why not"

We spend an hour in the café, we didn't even complete all the homework, but I felt good. After the things that happened today, I needed to distract my mind.

"Hey, what's your birthday plan update?" I feel sick when I ask her about her birthday plans. Because usually, she plans the stuff with me, and I'm the first person she tells anything to. Maybe it's because we're getting older. We're getting matured. *We're falling apart.* I'm scared to grow up.

"Well, the party is at my house, and since its day after tomorrow, I will plan the managements today and tell everyone tomorrow"

I stare at her for a while. Then smile. Not because of the party planning or stuff like that, but because she just included me in *everyone*. I wanted to ask her that, *why not this time?*

We used to plan things together, why not this time?

You didn't invite me, because you always knew I was the first to arrive, why not this time?

You rarely used the word 'I' and used 'us' or 'we' instead, why not this time?

"Sage?" she snaps her fingers. I just realized that I zoned out. "Don't forget to arrive at my house to help me in decorations, and stay up all night to clean the brutal mess, like you always do"

Oh my god, I'm such an over thinker. Again this time! I doubted Amy, again. I'm such an idiot.

I smile cheerfully and nod a yes.

It was time to leave because dad would kill me if I'm late.

I enter my house, just to find it empty. Mom and dad must be at work. I lay down on the couch, and for the next ten minutes, I just lay down there. I kept staring at the ceiling fan. I raised both of my hands up, then drop it back down. I felt weird, when tears started scrolling down my cheeks.

I'm going to fail, I'm going to get expelled, *I'm going to leave Amy.* I wasn't sobbing, but tears were still coming out.

I couldn't imagine going away from that someone who was always a part of you, someone who always listens to your stories, someone who accepted your flaws, someone who cries when you do and laughs when you do, someone who you never imagined to live without.

I will be leaving her. I will be forgetting about her. I will be living without her. NO.

Stop this shit Sage, I just over think, and all those things, that, *I just imagined.*

I finally stand up, to go to my room and change. When I open the door, I widen my eyes to find someone standing there.

"WHAT THE HELL DO YOU THINK YOU'RE DOING" I scream.

Sage

I feel cold on my right wrist. I scratch it. Then I felt hot. I thought the AC was on. I was sleeping on my bed, but it didn't felt like my bed. I again feel air pass my right wrist, I scratch it again………..wait, how am I scratching my wrist…………my bracelet?

I open my eyes, and what I saw, made me scream.

There were tons of people just staring me. There were almost ten people. They looked normal to me. But this isn't Blair's house. It was a large, white colored, modern house. I was sleeping on a bed with grey bed sheet. I look at my hand, and my bracelet wasn't there. I felt happiness and confusion at the same time. I was happy to no longer have the thing on, but I was confused how?

Oh, I might be dreaming again! I pinch my cheeks to wake myself up, but I didn't wake up. I looked up at the ceiling and yelled "TREV WAKE ME UP!" but there was no response.

Maybe, I'm not dreaming. Where am I? I looked at the people as they look at me puzzled. Then a lady said to a man "What is wrong with her? Is she even a human" Ugh that was offensive. Then another lady who looked really sweet, told me "Valerie, please don't scream my dear"

WHO IS SHE TO TELL ME NOT TO SCREAM FOR HELP?

AND WHO IN THE HOLY BISCUITS IS VALERIE?

"Valerie, don't panic, you just got hit in my head by a crazy man" said an old man. Who hit me in the head? And if I was hit in the head, why am I here and not with Blair and Trevor? Who are these people and why are they referring me as Valerie? Who is Valerie?

I think they kidnapped me……did they? Now they will cut my limbs and sell them for money, or maybe they will call my parents and ask them for money. I started crying aloud like a little baby "Ah please leave me! I am so young right now! My parents aren't rich! I want to go home! I have dreams to accomplish"

All of them stared me with a weird expression. I stopped crying because now I feel embarrassed. "Valerie, what are you talking about, and why are you acting so weird?"

I'M NOT ACTING WEIRD AND I'M NOT VALERIE.

I swear they're gonna kill me, they are scaring the living shit out of me. I jump out of the bed, and started running around "TREVOR HELP ME! BLAIR HELP!" I screamed in hope of getting attention from people outside.

Then suddenly someone grabs my shoulder and turns me around to face him. When I look at him, I'm enchanted with his blue eyes.

Blue eyes filled with ocean.

I got a sense of relief when I saw him. And I started crying "Clyder! H-help, I d-don't know where a-am I" He places his palms to my ears and whispered to me "its okay, calm down" then he turns to the people and exclaimed "You guys! She isn't aware, don't scare her, and stay away"

What does he mean by I'm not aware? My head is hurting so bad because of all this confusion. Then suddenly I heard someone scream

"Sage! Sage!!" I look around as to find the person who actually knows me. Then I felt dizzy, and I fainted. I could only see myself on the floor and Clyder trying to help me.

***

I open my eyes, to find a different room. I saw two people standing against the wall. Then I felt someone touching my wrist, I look around to find a lady, she was wearing a white coat, and on her neck hung a pair of…………stethoscope?

I'm in a hospital! I tried to open my eyes wide as the doctor said "Oh you're awake" Blair and Trevor quickly turn to me, and Blair sprinted to me and gave me a soft hug "Oh my god Sage, I was so scared about what happened to you"

I was again so confused but I don't want to question anything. I feel nauseous and I won't understand anything. I look around to see if Clyder's here or not, but he wasn't here.

The doctor gave me some medicine, and after I felt good enough to walk on my own, we left for home in a short while.

Trevor helped me sit in the back seat of the car and put my seat belt on. As we started driving, I asked "how did I end up here" Trevor sighs and says "Finally you asked, well, you fainted"

I know that I fainted but, how did they get to me in that weird house. Blair says "You were fainted in the kitchen"

What? Our kitchen? But how is that possible? Trev questions "And you were murmuring someone's name, was it Valemy?"

"No dummy, it was Valerie. Who's Valerie though?" Blair says.

Now everything makes sense. I was actually dreaming! I knew it. I dream so hard that I can't even wake up on pinching myself. And once again, I saw Clyder in my dreams. I look on my wrist, and yes, the bracelet is still there.

"Just a random friend" I lie. I don't even know who's Valerie?

Sometimes I really question my existence. Am I real? Am I actually alive or is this all a dream? What if I'm in a coma and just imagining stuff? Well I don't really think so. My life could be way better if I didn't have this bracelet on, or didn't get weird dreams. Should I be thankful to have such an interesting life, or should I cry about being the most confused person alive?

So many things were running through my mind, but the one which bothered me the most was Clyder's. He said that I'm not aware. But about what? What am I unaware of? The dream? Clyder is so random, in the dreams, and in real life. Speaking of real life, it's been weeks since I last saw Clyder. I pray everyday to find him again. When I was with him last time, I didn't want to tell him about my dream stuff. What if he thinks I am lying? Or what if he finds me a weirdo?

It's so strange how a man is nameless. I want to believe that he was lying about it, but I just can't, I'm unable to do it. I look at Blair and ask "Is it normal for a person to be nameless for as long as they can remember?" Trevor laughs on hearing this question. I'm annoyed by his laugh because it might be a funny question to them, but not for me, at least for now. "It depends" she says, and then keeps quiet for a few seconds because she was thinking something, then again says "People can be nameless if they have amnesia, or they're dumb, or maybe when they're parents are idiots to forget to name they're child"

I don't know if that was really helpful but eh.

I look outside the window, it was night, almost our bedtime but I didn't felt sleepy at all. The sky looked stunning, full of stars, as if someone had sprinkled a handful of iridescent opal dust against a velvet cloak.

When I again think about Clyder, I smile because I found it so cool that I named him, and he liked the name. I still don't know how I got the name on my tongue so suddenly.

Are there two Clyders though? One Clyder from my dreams and the other from the real world. The Clyder in the real world has an interesting story, appealing flashbacks and he doesn't seem to know me already. But the dream Clyder acts like I've known him forever, and he already knew my name, but he is weird.

Last time I saw him, he told me not to come up to him and not to hurt myself. And this time he said that I'm not aware. None of these made sense to me.

It's not normal to find someone in your dreams before you find them in real life.

I really want therapy. But the reason I don't, is that I've seen multiple therapists before, and they didn't find anything weird. And my mom always advised me not to go to therapy. My mom and dad are always hiding stuff from me. But one day, I'll get to the bottom of this.

This is my biggest aim in life, to know the truth that my parents are hiding from me. When I was young, these weird dreams and nightmares frightened me. I remember when I was thirteen; I used to cry so hard because of these dreams. I called Amy at midnight and told her how scared I was, she used to comfort me so much and never complained about how

I disturbed her sleep.

Suddenly I felt like my eyes were burning. They were actually filling up. I was..............crying? Ugh, it sucks to be so sensitive.

Being sensitive is like crying because an ant bit you. I don't even know what is the reason of me crying? Amy, Clyder or my fate with this bracelet?

Sometimes being sensitive isn't even that bad, it helps you dump your brain. I saw Trevor look at my crying face in the front mirror, he just blinked at me, assuring me that, it's okay to cry.

It's totally okay to cry sometimes, you just need to let everything out. Take out all the tension, stress, thoughts, depression and pain. It's absolutely okay sometimes for us not to be okay. We don't cry because we're weak, we do it because we've been strong for too long.

I wipe away my tears, and then close my eyes to take a moment to practice gratitude. Gratitude actually helps so much, it's helps me realize how lucky I am.

I have amazing cousins.

My parents love me.

I have a roof above my head and a job.

I have a sister who is in Stanford.

I have Taylor swift on my phone.

I got a new friend that I named myself.

But I don't have Amy.

I open my eyes quickly. I wanted to cry again. I want to meet her once again, just one last time, and tell her how much I loved and appreciated her. One last time, I want to hug her and remind her of the moments we had together. I want to look in her shiny brown eyes again. I want to hold her hand and tell her how much I miss her, even if this doesn't matter now. I want to cry to her and scream at her to express how I feel. She might be the last person I expected to leave me. A part of me doesn't want to believe that she did that intentionally and was forced to, just like she told. But the other part of me wants to stab her on her leg. Wants her life to be ruined. Wants her to choke to death. And tell her that I don't need her.

But actually I do.

Trevor opens the car door for me. I flinch because I didn't even realize that we reached home. I grab my stuff as I walk out of the car to the front door. But suddenly I don't want to go inside, even though I'm in the house now. I look around, then think about how my life could have been something else. I could have been to a better University like Stanford. I could have started my own business. But I lost my confidence after I dropped out of school. My life could have been something else, something bigger, something better, if I just studied harder, or maybe if I just didn't punched Chloe, or maybe if I didn't trusted Amy. I could have my own house, own car, and I could buy my parents one too. And I could have helped Lyn with her University.

I look back at Blair, then smile at her, secretly thanking her for letting me stay with them.

My mind has been thinking about so much and I'm dizzy now. I went to my room and literally threw myself on my bed with the back flat. I switched off my phone because I don't wanna get any notifications or call to disturb me. I don't feel sleepy at all, but I close my eyes to just switch off my brain and not think of any complications of my life.

I stay like this in the same position for the next ten minutes, and then

I finally felt a little better, mentally and physically. I heard a knock on my door; I raised my head to look who it is. It was Trevor.

"Are you okay? He asks me, sitting on the corner of my bed "What were you doing in the kitchen that had you fainted?"

The last thing I remember is that I was sitting on the couch watching Netflix on TV. Then I realized that I felt dizzy. It was because I hadn't ate anything for a very long while and also overworked, as I was so busy. When I finally got time, I sat down to watch TV then realized I needed to eat something. I went to the kitchen to make myself something to eat, but fainted.

"I overworked, and didn't ate anything so," I said in a faint voice, still audible to him. I sit straight, and look down at my legs. He asks me again with concern in his tone "Did you had those weird and terrible dreams again?" I nod, looking again at him. Then we kept quiet for a while. I suddenly felt like I should talk to him about moving out "Trev, I want to move out" he looks at me with a shocking expression. I realized I never saw him shocked before which is laughable "Move out? Why so suddenly? We're doing so well together. Is there something wrong?" I nod a no aggressively "Absolutely not, I actually love being here. But, you know, I always wanted to live on my own" then I smile "Well, I always wanted to start my own business." He smiles faintly then says "I kind of like the idea, so why not just do it!? Let's get to planning!" he stands up in excitement. Blair comes hearing Trev's enthusiasm. She gestures her hands, asking what's up. "Drink up coffee, we're working all night" he says to Blair. Wow, that was so out of the blue.

I laugh aloud, and I'm so glad that they're supporting me in my decision. I quickly pick up my phone, switch it back on and text my mom.

Me: I have a surprise for you :D

Few years ago

I snatch my diary from her hands and yell at her "Evelyn! Who the hell gave you the right to touch my stuff?" She folds her arms and tilts her head towards the side "I'm your sister, so yes, I do have the right. And perhaps, if you're so possessive, why don't you hide your damn stuff"

I keep my journal inside my drawer and point a finger at her "Because I'm used to being the only child" I turn away from her and walk towards my bed to charge my phone.

She comes and sits on my bed, and she knows I get annoyed by that. Even though she has her own bed in the corner of the room. She looks around, unsatisfied. "I don't want my room to be blue and filled with fangirly stuff, that's so cringe" Who does she think she is? She's only a year younger than me. I so want to punch her face, even though I know my fist will be hurting bad and mom will ground me.

"You mean *our* room, where I live more than you, and am allowed to paint it however I want" I added, backing her off. She rolls her eyes, stands up to leave, but she turns around and looks at me "I know what you and Amy did today"

My body stops functioning, and my hands started trembling. I slowly look at her, while she's smirking. Maybe she's talking about something else "What are you trying to say? Be open" I say confidently, not trying to look suspicious so she believes she's misunderstanding. "Sage, I'm in the piano club too"

Shit.

I stare at her without saying anything. I was panicking inside.

She's gonna tell mom and dad, she's gonna tell Emma, she's gonna tell the teachers. She's going to blackmail me, and I won't be able to stop her.

This day can't get any worse.

I don't even know how to react to this. Ashamed? Angry? Devastated? I don't know, so I wait until she speaks again "Why did you do that, I swear you weren't like this. That Amy made you do shits didn't she?" I look at her bitterly, and then said, clenching my teeth "Stop hating on Amy for no damn reason! She was never like this and never will be. She's a good person, instead, she tried to stop me. Plus, why should I really share my matter with you? Amy was, is, and will be better than you, forever, Evelyn" She just stares at me furiously, then turns around to leave. She holds the door knob, but turns around to say something "You should know more than that, Forever is meant for memories, not people, Sage" She then slams the door on me and leaves.

Forever is meant for memories, not people.

I didn't knew she had such a deep thinking. That really hit me hard. It sounded pretty.....true, but I'm not sure if the condition applies for me and Amy.

I lay down on my bed. I'm so stressed out right now. So much happened today. I try to look for my bag, but I forgot that I left it on the couch. So, I stand up to go get it. Once I came out of my room, I hard a glass breaking sound from the kitchen. I ran to see what's happening.

It was Evelyn. "I'm s-so sorry, I'll p-pick it u-up" she trembled, staring at the broken pieces of the coffee cup on the ground. I sigh. When she started to pick them up, she got a cut. She mumbled an "ouch" under her breathe. I don't understand why in the holy biscuits is she so clumsy. Like literally, all the freaking time, she's lumbering. And I bet that 'sorry' is her most used word ever.

As much as I want to go help her, I don't. Because I know that her 'sorry' will soon turn into 'shut up' or 'get lost'. She always hurts herself physically, unintentionally, everyday. I feel bad but, I know I will also feel like slapping her for the next few days.

I pick up my bag, and storm off to my room. I sat down on my desk, to write down my journal. It's like my daily habit. I've never missed a day. It's like my mind already knows that after coming from school, I must sit down to write.

I open it, take my pen, and get ready to express my emotions and bleed on paper. So many things happened today, I might fill up the whole notebook in one sitting. But I don't want to remember what happened today, and I also don't feel like writing. So I just wrote,

Dear Diary,

Today might be the most interesting day of my life, except my last birthday because that was legit insanely crazy. Today was interesting but, not in a good way. I don't even want to express anything, so I hope I burn this page, and all memories related to this day.

That's it. Then I close it. I stand up to put my journal back inside my bag, when I noticed something.

It was a book, but it wasn't mine. I looked at the cover and, it was a witchcraft novel. Oh, it's Amy's book.

She accidently put this books in my locker, it usually happened because she always takes my textbooks and notebooks, retouching makeup, and more from my locker without me getting noticed, and I do the same.

I reach out for my phone to call Amy and tell her that I have her book, or else she'll be panicking to lose her current favorite book.

I call her. Ringing…………… still ringing…………still ringing…………and………she didn't picked up. What? Oh well, I'll call her again.

Ringing…………Ringing……….and……….Declined? Why did she decline? I call her again almost immediately. It keeps ringing until………………..She picks up.

"Hello Amy? You there?" I heard nothing from the other side. But then I heard something crash, then I heard someone yelling at someone else. And after a few seconds, I heard someone sob, and that person was near the phone, almost on the call.

Oh no, Amy.

My heart sank when I understood what's going on. I just know exactly what's going on there. I can't believe it's happening again.

I thought of nothing and my mind went black. And the next second, I thought I might just leave to her. I was mumbling things to myself and I don't even know what. I don't want to see Lyn's face, and I can't leave Amy knowing what's happening there.

While I ran outside, I heard Evelyn "Where are you going!?" then I also heard her fall down. I really didn't bother to look around at her. So I didn't.

Sage

I open my eyes when I felt sun rays on my eyes. I suddenly felt dizzy when I try to move. Then I remember that I went to hospital last night. Last night was pathetic.

The weird dream.

Weird people.

Valerie.

Clyder.

I fainted.

In the kitchen.

Hospital.

My business.

Oh, yeah, I slept late. We slept late. I raise my head and found Blair sleeping on my desk, and Trevor sleeping on the floor. There were three empty cups on the table and a notebook near my head. We were planning my product. It was going to be cosmetics.

I flinch when Trevor suddenly yawns and opens his eyes "Oh, Ugh, good morning" he sits straight and stretches his arms. I rub my eyes as they are blurry. We both kept quite for a few seconds. Then Blair wakes up, she took her phone to check the time. She then casually says in a low voice "We're late for work" Trevor blinks hard then moves his shoulders

"Oh well" then stands up and leaves the room.

I fall back down on my bed as I feel lightheaded. Blair picks up the empty cups and says "Let's have a day off today, and go grocery shopping" Blair says, at a snail's pace. Trevor opens the door and says irritated "No, I'm not getting out of the house, I'm too tired"

"We barely have anything in the fridge, you are coming with us Trev" Blair says making an ugly face at him. He rolls his eyes and stomps away.

After a good half-n-hour, I come downstairs and find Trevor wearing his shoes "Let's go, we're having breakfast at Taco bell"

Oh yes! I don't remember the last time I had those mouth-watering grilled tacos and burritos. I wish we would go there on every weekend but, we need to save money and not spend them on tacos.

The only thing scared me that I wore a white off shoulder and I don't know how but a stain is enforced to have on that very day. Blair was smart enough to wear a black T-shirt tucked in flare jeans.

On our way, Blair looks at Trevor and says "Did you tell her" he looked confused so he asked "Tell her what?"

"Come on, don't act in the clear" she lightly punches him on the shoulder. I look at them all confused. It wasn't a bad news because Blair was smiling. "Okay let me tell her. Sage, you know how Trevor has been very busy with his phone and has been outside more than usual?" I raise an eyebrow "Yea?"

Before Blair even told me, realization slapped me. I screamed "Oh my goodness Trev!!" Blair starts laughing and I do too.

"W-why are you guys laughing? Sage you know nothing, I-" he says but I interrupt him "You're dating someone?" then I started laughing even more.

Blair tries to stop laughing and says "Yes! This guy is dating a girl!" I chuckle and asked him "Trev, was that girl blind?"

"No, why?"

"Then how did she like an idiot-face like yours?" We both started laughing again while Trevor kept driving with a dull expression.

Damn, never in my life did I thought a man like Trevor dating. I knew he was going to date a girl soon, but I didn't saw it coming so out of the blue.

I got so curious and keyed up to have a sister-in-law in our family "So like, when are you getting married?"

Trevor looks at me in the front mirror with his eyes widen, then Blair started to laugh once again.

"MARRIAGE? Are you serious? It's only been five months!"

"Liar!" Blair says. "You and that girl are friends since three years, but then you guys started dating an year ago" That's interesting.

"Eh, a year is enough though" I say looking out the window, as Trevor parks the car at the place.

The restaurant wasn't very crowded so it felt peaceful. We sit down and order our meals. "What would you like to have, Sir"

"We'll have a Sausage Flatbread melt and a steak and egg burrito, and Sage?"

I actually came here for a burrito but the tacos looked delicious "I'll have some Doritos Locos Tacos and three cups of coffee for each of us"

"Alright, I'll be back with your food in a couple of minutes." Then he leaves. We're getting a delicious meal after a very long time and it's so pleasant.

"So Trev, tell us about that girl" I smirk at Blair. "Ugh, why are ya'll so nosey, anyways, so, she's a medical practitioner"

"Oh, a doctor" Blair says, impressed "What's her name?" Trevor giggles under his breath. I wanted to laugh so hard at him. "Well, why don't you guys meet her yourselves, that will make you guys closer" I look at Blair and she does too, thinking the same thing that, since when did he become so thoughtful?

But another thing that comes to my mind is that, I could have been a qualified high educated student, if I worked a little harder, and could have been less attached to Amy. Whenever I hear about people being so successful like a doctor or an entrepreneur, I wished I could be like one too. I would have gone to a business school. Not that I was jealous, it's just a thought.

I snap out of my thoughts and looked around. What I find strange is that a part of me wants to find Clyder here. It's like I want to talk to him again, right now. He gives off really good vibes, when I stood beside him, it felt like he gives off a non-perfume fragrance that smells better than any other perfume.

I move my eyes around, as if I'm going to meet his eyes. I met dark black eyes, siren eyes, deep brown eyes, sparkling hazel eyes, adorable big eyes, oceanic blue eyes…………wait, are those………

Blue eyes filled with ocean.

Holy biscuits! What in the world is he doing here? He's standing at the counter; it doesn't look like he's here for food. Why is he here then? He turns around to my table. I quickly lift the menu book up to hide my face.

I know I said I wanted to meet him, but not here, not in front of Blair and Trevor.

I can feel him staring at me. I hope he didn't recognize me. I saw him leave the place. I left a huge sigh of relief. Trevor looks at me with a ridiculous expression on his idiot-face. Did he notice me hiding from him? He raises an eyebrow at me, I just roll my eyes and look down at my phone. I'm not actually going through my phone, I'm just typing random numbers on the calculator. It reminds me of something funny. When sometimes I went to family events, I always had social anxiety and suffocation in the crowd. And I wanted to avoid talking to any person at that time, so I texted Amy random letters and she always used to laugh and say that she knew why I'm texting her nonsense.

I was so busy with typing numbers that I almost didn't realize that the food arrived, and I also realized that my stomach was growling.

Without wasting any time, I dig in. I feel a little sense of regret. Maybe I should walked up to him to say a hi, or at least wave my hand at him. I don't even know why I'm hiding Clyder from Trevor and Blair. He's just a friend. Who I named myself? Is it even normal to make a nameless boy your friend because you feel like you know him? What if he is lying and will kidnap me for money? What if he kills me? How can I make a stranger my friend for no reason? I'm so weird.

But at the time when I talk to him, I forget these things, I don't question anything. I listen to him as if it's my own problems, and as if I know how to solve them. He looks at me as if he's talking to someone so deeply for the first time. Well, I mean, he did tell me that he doesn't really have anyone to talk to. If I knew where he lived, maybe I could buy him groceries, helping as a friend. Maybe get him a job, and so much more.

But why do I care? He's like nothing to me. I'm not even sure if he refers me as his friend. Does he think about me the way I do? I bet he doesn't even remember the name I gave him.

"Oh my gosh Sage, why do you always zone out" Trev boomed, making me flinch. I just realized that they were having a conversation and I was supposed to hear it. I blame Clyder for this one.

"Yeah, um, so what were we talking about?" I asked, taking the last bite of my Taco. "Your business, silly" Blair says with a goofy smile on her face. "What do you plan to name it?"

What do I plan to name it? I don't know. What can I name it that goes along perfect with cosmetics and skincare products? No clue, at all. I'm always bad at naming things.

"No idea yet, but you know what, lets give ourselves a little more time to come up with the best ideas"

I pick up my phone to check the notifications. A message from my mom,

Mom: Surprise? What can it be?

I smile and text her back.

Me: It's called a surprise for a reason!

Few years ago

I was out of breath speed walking for straight five minutes. I reached her house and saw her mom's car in the garage. That means her mom is home early.

I sneaked around the house and reached her window. It was closed so I knocked on it. I couldn't hear anything. After I knock a little louder, the window opens immediately. I look through the window to find Amy standing there. She wasn't crying, but her eyes were red and puffy. Her room was a clear mess. There were pieces of glass on the floor and the pillows were thrown around. She was still in those clothes that she wore to school. Her bag was on the ground near the wall, as if someone threw it to hit someone. The spot was brutal.

After roaming my eyes around, I look back at Amy. She had tears in her eyes. She inhaled a long breathe and asked me exhaling "What are you doing here?" then she gives me her hand so that I could climb in her window. This wasn't new because sometimes I sneak in her house without her mom knowing because as I said, she hates me in her house, she hates me for no damn reason.

I jumped inside "What happened here" I asked her dodging her question, even though I knew what happened. She looks down as tears drop from her eyes. I pull her in a very light and slow hug. She was shaking in fear, I know she had a panic attack.

"Why?" I asked in a very faded voice. "She came to know that I was planning my birthday"

Oh my holy biscuits. That's it? I can't imagine the rage Ms. Darren must have had. She probably hit Amy so much, I could see the bruises. "Now she's not leaving the city ever without me"

"It doesn't matter if the party cancelled, no one cares Amy, are you okay?" in what world does a mother hit her daughter for celebrating her birthday?

She nods and says "Thank you so much" I couldn't help myself so I teared up. I can never imagine what she has to go through everyday. Sometimes I wish her dad was here. No dad would like to see her daughter in pain. No mother likes to hurt her daughter too, well, Ms. Darren is an exception.

I can't tell her that I understand, because I don't. I don't understand her pain, but I want to. I want to tell her that it's okay, but it isn't. It's not okay. But it is okay not to be okay, right?

Sometimes I wish that this was a dream, all of it.

I break the hug and look at her. Then I make her sit down on her bed. I look around at the messy room. The room was painted in a very faint pastel purple, almost looks like white, but giving a sense of purple. Her desk was messy with her books and pens. The wall near her bed was filled with the posters of her favorite witch land series. My eyes fall on her feet. There were small glass pieces stuck on her foot and it was bleeding. I immediately look around to find a first aid box. I try my best to be silent so her mom wouldn't know that I'm here. I go through her drawers and found it. I sit down on the floor and start to carefully take out the pieces.

"Sage…"

"Yeah?" I said, still focusing on her foot.

"Why did you come here?"

I sigh "I came, so now, don't you dare tell me that I didn't had to"

She keeps quite for a while and then says "I won't, because you had to, I needed you" I look up at her, then smile. After I cover up her foot, I sit beside her on the bed.

"Do you feel better now?" I ask her, lying down on her bed. She nods and lies beside me. "Maybe you should go home now, you're being too good, I can't thank you enough for always being by my side"

I turn to her "I'm not going home right now, I don't want to. I'm better when I'm with you" I look towards the ceiling and close my eyes.

"Let me guess, Evelyn is home" I chuckle when she guesses it right. "You know me so well"

She chuckles too "Why do you hate her so much, she's not that bad, sometimes I feel bad for how clumsy she is" I look back at her, then sit straight and state "Look, I don't hate her, I just don't understand why did she had to leave her own family? She visits us only when she wants. She doesn't understand the value of a family. And about her being clumsy, it's so stupid. She always hurts herself accidently. Right now before coming to you, she broke a cup and also sprained her ankle. The way she screamed, I think she hurt herself bad. Mom and dad will literally kill me when I get home"

She laughs. I'm relieved that she's laughing. "That's bad, poor Evelyn. But that's factual that we shouldn't take our family for granted"

I don't understand why Amy's always so sweet to Evelyn, while she talks rubbish about her.

"Okay but Sage, you really need to get going, your parents might wonder where you are" she says, sitting straight. "Okay, but first, let me help you clean this mess. And Amy, I promise, your birthday isn't gonna be ruined, it won't be a blast but, I will do whatever I can" I smile.

Sage

"Did you really think it was a good idea to come back here?"

"I wanted to risk it for the biscuit" Trevor parks the car at the store.

"What type of biscuit dummy? After what you did here last time, he will kick your ass out" I said, putting my phone inside my purse.

"Trev, we can have fun somewhere else but this shopkeeper will call the police if you break more eggs"

"Oh come on, how bad can it possibly be?" he exclaimed "Let's go cause some chaos."

He is literally going in that store again. He said he's intentionally gonna break an egg to annoy the shopkeeper, well, I know he's probably kidding because, he can't be that stupid. Right?

We all enter the store. Our eyes roam around to look for the shopkeeper, but he was no where to be seen. Then suddenly a person appears from behind the shelves. He had visibly brown eyes and blonde hair. He was wearing glasses and an open black shirt layered on a white T-shirt. He had headphones hung on his neck.

My eyes were staring at his neck that was filled with tattoos. Even his left arm. He looked like a random customer just like us.

"Can I help you?" his voice was so striking. "Hey man, have you seen that cranky old shopkeeper?" Trevor says, still looking around. I don't even know why we're looking for the shopkeeper, to mock him? Trevor's being hilariously evil.

"Cranky?" the guy raises his eyebrows, and then moves his eyes towards Blair, then again to Trevor "What do you mean by cranky old shopkeeper?"

"Dude, just tell me if you know where he is, because I bet you find him as annoying as we do" that was funny but I didn't felt any laughter coming up my throat. The guy starts popping his knuckles, then cracks his head and says "You can talk to me about whatever you wanna talk about" he stares deep in Trevor's eyes.

Trevor looks at me and whispers "Do you think he left his brain in the bathroom?" I chuckle. Then we heard the bathroom door open, and the old shopkeeper appears.

He widen his eyes and yells in a very *old-person* voice "Hey! That guy! He is that mischievous egg breaker" I look at Blair, she looks back at me. Then we both stare at Trevor.

"Really dad?" says the guy. I gulped when I heard him say that. Trevor's jaw drops and he points at the shopkeeper then the other guy. That guy smiles and says "And I'm the son of the *cranky old shopkeeper*" Trevor gulps and sighs to me "I guess ya'll were right" then he tilts his head towards Blair "This really wasn't a fun idea"

The guy didn't really look friendly. Is there still time to run? We all kept staring at each other for the next few seconds while the guy kept glaring at Trev, grinding his teeth. Blair then takes a long breath and says "okay so now we got to leave" she then laughs awkwardly. The guy looks at Blair and says "Nope, not right now" then he starts to walk towards

Trevor, rolling up his sleeves. Blair states "Oh, not right now? Okay" Then again laughs awkwardly again, and then boomed "RUN!"

I was so out of my soul that I almost fell down when Trev and Blair ran, then I looked up at the guy, then realized, and I started to run behind Trevor. I was running so fast that I couldn't think of anything, and I could only see Trevor running in front of me. Trev kept looking behind me and Blair was just running towards the car mindlessly.

I can feel that man running behind us and yelling at us. I swear he runs like an athlete. We quickly sit in the car, but now Blair was sitting in the driver's seat. I swear that guy was like a gangster. Blair quickly drives out of the place.

We all were breathing heavily. I almost fainted. I close my eyes and rest my head on the window. Blair scolds Trevor "Yes I knew I was right. You're an idiot". Trevor and I broke into laughter. "What's so funny?" she says, glancing at Trevor.

"Everything dummy"

Okay but seriously, I don't remember the last time I laughed so heartily. I feel so light. Like I have nothing to worry about. Blair was smiling now. Sometimes I feel like cousins are way better than siblings. All Evelyn and I did was fight over the TV remote and the front seat of the car. And I don't remember any better memories because my own sister never wanted to stay with her family. I hate mom and dad for this. Why did they ever allow her to leave the house anyways?

And here's the twist, I know that there is some other reasons that she doesn't live with us. But don't know what. As I said, I might be the most confused human being ever.

"Can we get ice cream?" I asked Trevor.

"No"

"But it's been so long-"

"No"

"But we-"

"No"

"TREV"

"NO"

I really thought I had a chance….

We then enter another grocery store. Everything was stacked up. Blair keeps the car keys in her purse and says to Trev without looking up "Trev I was thinking that-" she looks up to find Trevor missing "Trev? Where did he go?" and I just realized that my eyes were on the ice cream corner the whole time so I didn't see Trev.

We really didn't think much about it because he's probably where he loves to be, the cereal sections. Then Blair and I did what we always loved to do.

I secretly pointed at a random girl by tilting my head and asked Blair "Do you really think green's her color?"

"definitely not, she'd be way better in pink"

"Okay but like what type of pink?"

"Probably hot pink or magenta"

"Hot pink or fuscia for me. Speaking of me, does red suit me?" I say pointing at my red shorts.

"Ah, girl! Definitely! Amaranth is the best for you. I totally love your light corals too"

"Omg same!"

We kept talking till we realized that we're just roaming around. "Do me a favor Blair…"

"Yea?"

"Keep me away from the candy section"

She chuckles on me. No but I'm serious. I love chocolates. Like, so very much.

Blair was moving the shopping cart. We were looking for bread. Brown bread. "Why do they only have white bread- Oh wait I found it!" she keeps a pack "where are the waffles?"

After picking some stuff from this one corner, we're heading to the dairy section. I stopped mid way when I found Trev, exactly where we expected him. The cereal section.

He turns to me and says "Sage look, they have Cinnamon Toast Crunch" I raise an eyebrow at him and walk towards him.

I roam my eyes around to look for other cereals. They seriously had so many. Cheerios, lucky charms, frosted flakes "And look, they also have Cap'n Crunch!"

He looks at me with a disgusted face "Cap'n Crunch? Seriously? More like Commodore Crunch"

"At least it's better than that Cinnamon roll or whatever you call it"

"IT'S CINNAMON TOAST CRUNCH, YOUNG LADY"

"AND I SAID WHATEVER, SIR"

"Are ya'll again fighting over cereals?" Blair walks casually between us. "We're getting both, idiots"

Blair already got milk and butter. We all just roam around looking at the stuff. Trev stops when he sees, none other than, coffee. While Blair was just looking for her favorite type, he opened the cap and started to smell them. "Stop, you're disgusting"

We might end up in a big mess, I just have this gut feeling. Trevor picks up a random box, and there was Japanese written on it so I couldn't tell what it was. It's not ramen though. Trevor points at the box and says "Can we get this? It looks so delectable"

"Why are you acting dumb" said Blair. "What do you mean dumb?"

"We both don't know how to cook that dumbass" and when she turns around, Trev looks at me. Then keeps that thing in the cart anyways. Then I turn around when I see that half of the store is empty. An employee walks beside me "Hey, are you guys closings already? Isn't it too early?" I asked.

"Oh, yes actually, we've got some issues so we're closing early" then he walks away. I turn around and start to punch Trevor's shoulders "TREVOR THEY'RE CLOSING!"

He flinches and keeps his hand on his chest "Jeez Sage! So what?!"

"WE NEED TO HURRY!"

He stares at me as if I just threw up on him. "Hey kiddo lets go already" he says to Blair. She nods and starts walking towards the counter. The line was pretty long, AND THAT HAD ME PANICKING. I kept popping my knuckles and rubbing my palms in anxiety. "What if they close and we get trapped here?!"

"Have you lost it?"

Blair was checking the stuff to see if she's got everything or not "Damn it, we forget the chips"

"We'll get it" Trev says. What does he mean by *we?* They're closing already and we didn't get all the items? That's so careless. I feel sassy right now, weird. Trevor takes the cart and moves out of the line "Why are you taking the cart?"

"Because you never let me move the cart, I like doing it…."

Blair leaves a big sigh. We're so done with him. "Stay in the line while we come back" but I don't wanna go.

But I start walking with him anyway. "Listen Trev, we need to hurry up, they're closing"

He smirks and says "Oh yeah? Watch me" then he starts running fast with the cart. I swear he's out of his mind. He's gonna break a bone, I can tell. I run after him. "Blair will kill you if continue to do everything but buy chips"

"Whatever" he says looking behind. And guess what, something happened which wasn't really supposed to happened. The cart's wheel screwed down- I mean it broke. And Trevor crashed into a stack of canned beans.

I won't even act surprised, I already knew it. I won't hide my mad face to Trevor, but I really wished I wasn't becoming a red tomato out of embarrassment. Right now I want to clap sarcastically and scold him so bad but, WE DON'T HAVE TIME THEY'RE CLOSING.

"Stand up we need to leave!" I yell at him. He stands up and groans "Why are you panicking? It's really not a big deal" Oh yes it is, or maybe not, I don't care.

Then his phone starts ringing and It's Blair, that means we need to reach to her fast.

GOD I'M NEVER COMING GROCERY SHOPPING WITH THEM

AGAIN.

We literally ignore the mess and run away like we're never coming back here.

Blair yells at us "Are you guys kids? You got to be kidding me! Whatever, give me your wallet and forget about the chips"

Trevor nods and starts checking his pocket for his wallet, then he gulps and curses under his breathe. I stare at him with my eyes widen. "Well, I um-"

"TREV HOW CAN YOU FORGET?" Blair yells.

If that wasn't enough, an employee comes "Sir, do you mind cleaning up the mess you just created? Or else you got to pay"

Yes, definitely never coming back here.

Few years ago

"Evelyn! Give me my phone back!" I was hunting her around the house. I picked up a pillow and threw at her. "Before I turn this into a pillow fight, hand me over my phone"

"And what if I don't?" she tosses my phone into the air, then catches it and starts fidgeting. I want to yell at her so bad right now, but I don't wanna get into trouble. "Look, Lyn, what do you want?" I ask her very calmly.

"I know you're going out to hang out with Amy" How does she know everything I do all the time? Is she an undercover agent or something? "Okay, yeah, so what?"

She smiles widely, exposing her white shimmering teeth and beamed "So take me with you!"

I hissed "What the hell, why would I do that?" she sighs loudly and sits down on the couch, then crosses her legs. "Because you know that mom doesn't want me to be close to you" she says miserably.

That's actually true. Mom really acts like she hates us together. She never said that but, her actions speak louder. She always sets different plans for us when she has the chance, as if she doesn't want us collectively. She even wanted different schools for us, but failed to get me anywhere else but this school. She begged us not to hang out together much often.

Me and Evelyn really hated her for this but, we trusted her. We knew that whatever she's doing is just for our good, and she'll tell us when she's ready, at the right time.

"I don't want you with me, mom won't appreciate me being with you. Let's not be rascals for this, and listen to her" I state.

"I know, at least let me sneak out so mom won't know I'm out with my friends" she tosses back my phone "Okay but why don't you just go? Why do you wanna sneak out?"

She makes a jaded face and says "Because I'm grounded, Numbskull!"

Numbskull?! What the heck is that suppose to mean?

"What if I get in trouble?" she better have a good response for this. "What if I tell mom about how you almost killed Emma, at such a young age. So pathetic of you" She crosses her arms.

I don't want to respond back, but if I don't, that'll be bad. I press my palms to my forehead "It was nothing what it looked like, you're taking it too far"

She chuckles sarcastically "Yeah, right. I'll be back in about ten minutes" then she walks back to her room.

For the next ten minutes, I sat down on the couch and opened my phone.

Me: You ready?

Amy: I am but, you seriously don't have to do all this.

Me: This is the least I could. Now be there in twenty minutes. I hate waiting.

Amy: :)

I keep my phone on my lap, then just wait till Evelyn comes out. I know she doesn't do makeup so she won't take time.

She comes out of her room and just heads to the front door ignoring me. I stand up as she just walks past me. She opens the door and tilts her head "let's go."

We walk out that door as I realized that I had to walk myself to the place. "Don't tell mom, or else"

"I know, now go" She stomps of but stops middle way "Sage,"

"What is it?" she hesitates to speak so I move forward to ensure her that no one is around right now. "Well," she says "We need, a talk" I rolled my eyes and said "Are you serious? We ARE talking"

She makes an annoyed face and said furiously "No! I mean like a real talk, a serious one" I felt awkward. I pushed my hair back and said "What do you wanna talk about?"

She nods her head and says "No not right now, not like this. Later, maybe… "

She's annoying me. I just walk away from there. But like, what does she wanna talk about. She never talked to me like that. She's either annoyed, mad or guilty, when she breaks something because she is annoyingly clumsy. But this time I saw her anxious and afraid. This better not be a prank.

I just hate myself right now, because I forgot my earphones. I put my hands in my pocket and kept thinking about the morning I went through today.

When I woke up this morning, I was sweating. I was always breathing heavily. I didn't know why. Or maybe, I didn't remember why.

I probably saw a terrible nightmare. Once again. I think its okay to have nightmares or weird dreams but, is it really okay to have them everyday?

Most of the times I lucid dream. That's when I know that I'm in a dream.

Many people lucid dream but I feel like I'm the empress of lucid dreaming. Once I injured myself while dreaming. I fell down the stairs in my dreams and when I woke up, I was on the floor lifelessly. I felt like my body had fallen down from a cliff.

I stop by a bookstore. Dang it, I almost forgot to buy Amy or gift, I really am a Numbskull. But I have the perfect gift idea for her.

As I enter, my eyes lit up. I wanted to scream "Holy biscuits!!" but that would be quite embarrassing.

I walked around and for the next five minutes, I'm totally distracted by so many books. Right now I wanted to buy all of them, like the whole section. But I'm technically broke. I only have enough pocket money to buy her two books. I can buy three but I want to save money for food.

I moved to the fantasy sections and, oh my holy biscuits. It was organized as heaven. I mean I know it is supposed to be organized anyways but like, the colors are so fascinating. I had a sudden interest in fantasy now, and I so want to open each and every book here. But I broke out of my thoughts when I got a text.

Amy: Where are you?

Oh damn, I almost forgot. I rush and pick two books of her favorite author.

I was out and I reached there in no time. She was at a bus stop, no we're not taking any bus. She looks at me frustrated.

"What took you so long?" she say, irritated. I just smile at her and move the bag of books towards her "Happy birthday"

She gives me a very warm smile. Then she takes the bag and realized what I gifted her. She looks at me in delighted, with a little shock. "You bought me books?"she says "Sage! I told you that you didn't have to!"

I roll my eyes and say "I know, but I did that because my mom didn't allow me to take anyone to watch movies, so this book is a replacement of the movie tickets. But! I will be buying us lunch, I don't have enough money for a cake…..we can cut a cupcake if you want" She laughs. I feel so good knowing that I'm making her day better by making her laugh.

We start walking when I ask her "Amy," I hesitate "Do you mind if I ask something?"

"Oh my god, this is the first time you're asking me if you can ask a question or not, or else you're always a doofus" I look at her in disgust "What the hell, shut up. Alright so, did your mom say anything about what happened after I left that day?"

She throws her head back, then places her hands on the back of her head and sighs "I didn't left my room that day. I sneaked out of my room once or twice to grab some food. But mom didn't come to check me even once. The next day, it was like she didn't even care what happened" then she looks at me "But you know what," she looks away "It doesn't effect me anymore"

I really shouldn't have asked this question, that was so bitter.

I just kept thinking about that, is Ms. Darren the reason why Amy's dad left? Or did he die when Amy was little? Her mom never told her. I know that I have no right to know about it, but I never had this thought in the first place when it comes to Amy. I refuse to believe that there is anything that Amy hides or lies about.

We took a table and started picking our orders. I realized I was struggling to pick an order, and I had a reason for that. The dream I saw last night, had disturbed my brain. I'm having a block. When Amy noticed me, she said "What dream did you have last night?"

I chuckle because it's funny how she realized it "I don't even remember, and I don't want to"

Amy takes out the books I bought her, and started reading the summary. It's just funny how we are casually ignoring the fact that I'm gonna get expelled, that's because we can't do anything about it. She still doesn't know that I'm going to move out the city, that's why she's chill. While she checked them out, I opened my phone and decided to text Evelyn if she reached there or not.

This might be the first time I'm being concerned about her. Maybe because of what happened earlier. After I texted her, I started scrolling through some social media.

"Sage, I swear that you accidently picked one of the best books" she was so happy. While scrolling, I came across a post regarding our school.

Who's ready for the competition? #Music

I look up and saw that our food had arrived. "Do you know about any sort of competition going on in our school?" I asked her, but she already stuffed food in her mouth.

"Competition?" she said, still chewing her food. She finishes her bite and says "I don't know" then takes another bite. She looks like a hungry bear.

I dig in too, ignoring the post. But then I got a notification from Mia. She is a friend of mine; we met when her and I paired up in a science project.

Mia: By any chance, do you still have my guitar with you?

Why does she want her guitar all of a sudden? I borrowed her guitar a few months ago because I love playing guitar. I play guitar since forever. I just do it because I love music. But I only play it in front of my parents and Amy. I lost mine so I borrowed hers because she was about to throw it away.

Me: What for? I thought you're bored of playing guitar?

Mia: I was, but I need it for the competition.

Me: What competition?

Mia: Music competition! Didn't you heard about it?

Oh. So our school is conducting a music competition. Good for Chloe, she might win, if Emma doesn't participate.

"What happened?" she says while I was staring at the texts. "Our school is conducting a music competition"

She looks at me with enchantment in her eyes "Oh my god, this is perfect!" she says, her hands making fists "This is the moment you show our school how talented you are"

"Amy, you know I'm not into playing guitar a lot now-a-days, and perhaps, I'm too stressed to do all this. Besides, you're an amazing singer, you should particip-"

"NO" she cuts me "Sage! Remember when I told you that you're my favorite musician? You still are, and my singing is nothing without your music"

I smile at how she's trying to motivate me, but it's of no use.

"That's right, you're singing really is nothing, with or without" someone says from my behind. I can tell that it's Chloe by the look on Amy's face.

"Happy birthday little princess! May your wishes come true" she says dramatically. I keep quite because I don't want to rumble with her or punch her again. "You must be getting paid for ruining people's day, that's why you're rich" Amy said. Since when did she start to think of such come backs?

"That was lame, birthday girl"

"Like you?"

Chloe took a seat with us. Surprisingly, she's not with her minions. She crosses her legs and just smiles. "Why are you here Chloe?" I ask her, trying to stay calm.

"I'm here with an offer" she throws her hair behind her back. Amy looks at me with a confused look.

"You know, to be honest, I feel stupid by telling my dad that you punched me and that will cause you to get expelled" Of course she feels stupid, not bad. Her voice doesn't sound sympathetic, it sounds sassy and overdramatic. She smiles like a psycho and says "So, I'm making a deal!"

Amy and I look at each other, so done with her. But maybe her deal would make sense and I won't fail. "And what's that?" Amy asked.

She leans in closer, placing her elbows on the table "You heard about the music competition, didn't you?" oh gosh, her deal is related to the competition. Alright, I can do this.

I nod. "If you guys, win the competition, ya'll are safe. But, if you guys lose, even on the second place, my dad will fail you and I'm gonna spread brutal rumors about you. That will cause your reputation to spoil, harshly." she smirks.

I don't care if she spreads rumors because if I drop out, I'm going out of town. But I don't want to drop out, I love my life in Ohio.

"Why are you making a deal?" I ask because I'm confused. She could have told her dad and ended this, but why did she give me a chance?

"Because I want to see you struggle," she says while her smile drops and she sits back straight. She takes a long breathe and says "All these years you've been in school, you're adjacent to me. Only you, you made people believe that I'm a scoundrel. You dared to stand up against me. You made me look like the bad guy." She sighs and continues "I want to see you move violently. I want to look at you when you mess up. I want to see you cry when you lose in opposition to me. You should be thankful that I gave you an opening"

I never knew she was so against me. I thought I never existed for her, but I guess I always pissed her off. I should be worried about it, but I wanna laugh. I'm so appreciative that I never let anyone knew that I play guitar. If Chloe already knew, she wouldn't dare to ask me.

She stands up and turns to Amy "Happy returns of the day" then turns around at the speed of light and sprints away.

"I wish she knew how stupid she sounded" beamed Amy. Then she sits straight eagerly and boomed "Sage! You're not gonna get expelled!" I laughed. She's so confident that I'm gonna win. "I haven't even won, how are you sure that I won't get expelled?"

She rolls her eyes and says "Because I never saw anyone play better than you" Well that's probably a lie and a very old way of complimenting. What matters the most is that, does she really mean it? And of course she does.

Music isn't my passion or ambition, it's just an interest. I could have been famous if my mom sent me to guitar lessons, but I never asked for it. I learned a little from here and there, kept playing for years and I guess it was just a hidden talent. I could have gone to international competitions or start a YouTube channel. Damn, there were so many things I could have done.

But I don't wanna be famous. I want to have a normal life. I will open my own company. I will buy myself all those things I dreamed of, and also meet Taylor. Amy and I will go out on weekends together. We will travel together. We both have our future plans ready. Only once, once I pass this grade, everything will be back to normal. I won't let anyone blackmail me, and I won't put any of us in a position to drop out.

Amy's phone suddenly starts buzzing. She picks it up. All I could here from the other side was someone yelling and being sarcastic. Then I heard that person say my name. That's definitely her mom.

She hangs up without saying anything. She looks at me and leaves a sigh. "You already knew who it was, didn't you?" I nod. She stands up and says "Got to go. Thank you so much, I really mean it." I smile. I was about to say something when she points a finger at me "Don't you dare spend another damn cent on my birthday so called surprise"

Then she smiles and waves a bye to me. I move in the opposite direction when she stops in the middle way and says "Sage! Tonight, my house at seven, guitar practice. Because I know you haven't played it for a while, I wanna hear you play"

"But I don't have a guitar anymore! Mia wants her back"

"I know, just arrive at my house. Trust me!" then she sprints away.

***

"Do you really think I'm that good?" I asked mom, while grinding chips and watching TV. "Of course you are. You're the only one in our family who plays guitar"

Evelyn got home later after I did, and the fact that mom still has no clue. "I have to visit Amy today, I'll be home at eight or nine"

"Didn't you just meet Amy this morning?" Evelyn interferes. Why does she have to be so nosey? "Yeah, but I have some work today, and I believe it's none of your business"

It's already four right now. And I just realized that Evelyn needed to talk about something. Just as I was about to ask her, I heard her scream. Me and mom turned around to find that she burned her hands severely while doing something in the kitchen.

"Oh my god! Honey! I told you to be careful" mom darts to here, picking her hand up. "I'm so sorry" she said.

I've had enough of her. First, she always hurts herself and is extremely clumsy. Then she apologizes for no damn reason to prove herself naive? What is wrong with her?

Sometimes I think she does this for attention. Whatever it is, I always see mom and dad being fearful for her.

I stand up and yell at her "Why can't you be more careful? Mom and dad always suffer because of you. You can't take care of yourself properly which always makes them worry about you all the time. And then you express regret? When will you grow up?"

"Sage! That's not how you speak to your sister"

"Yes I can, because she's being a moron"

"Stop, or else" moms says when Evelyn runs away to our room. Mom looks at me in disbelief "I never expected you to be so rude. You only act like a human being with Amy, or else you're monstrous"

Monstrous? Now mom is labeling me a monster, because of Evelyn. That's ridiculous. I stomp towards our room to have a talk with her.

I open the door to find her crying her heart out, burying her face in a pillow. I want to scold her and yell at her, I want to call her a dimwit on her face. But I just stare at her, while I blame myself. I came here to scold you, but my thoughts totally flipped looking at her.

All I ever learned from life is that, no matter what you do, just never, never ever break someone's heart. The tears she's spilling right now are because of me. I'm blaming myself for this, blaming me, my words, my actions and my emotions.

As a sister, I should be the one to comfort her. But instead, I'm the one who she need's to be away from. The negative thoughts of her made me so blind that I killed her with my words.

When she broke the cup and hurt her fingers, I should have helped her but instead, I ignored her. When she sprained her ankle, I should have picked her up but instead, I left her behind. When she burned her finger, I should have comforted her but instead, I yelled at her and called her a moron.

I really am being monstrous.

She raises her head to face me. I can see that she wants to scream at me, but words can't spill out of her lips right now. I don't want to apologize, but I should. This might be the first time me apologizing to her "Lyn, I'm sorry. I shouldn't have reacted this way. I know you don't want me here right now, I'll just leave"

"Yes, I want you to leave, but not right now" she sits up straight, wiping her tears up. I think she wants to talk, about the thing she wanted to. Is it related to what just happened?

I sit next to her, waiting for a response. "Sage, I am not clumsy on purpose for any attention. I don't mess up my balance and coordinates for interest." Then she hesitates to speak, but says "I have Dyspraxia"

What is that? What is Dyspraxia? I don't know why I'm panicking. It just doesn't sound right. It sounds scary and horrifying. It's not that major, is it?

My expression clearly shows fear. I felt like a thousand needles were pricking through my skin.

"I don't want to tell you any details about it. I chose you to open up to because, I feel like you will understand, because you're my sister"

This might be the first time she called me her sister, and I actually felt like her big sister.

She again buries her face in the pillow, but now she isn't crying. I cannot hold in my tears anymore so I run out.

I sit on the couch, rethinking about how I treated her. I pick up my phone and search, what is Dyspraxia? I felt helpless and tearful as I read.

Brain disorder

Movement difficulties

Marked by clumsiness

Rare

I have no clue how to react. I just sit there, very still. I am crying right now, but making no sound. I am a fiend for her. She never told us before, and we never noticed it, because she was never with us. And it was not her fault, none of it. I thought she's the culprit, but she was the victim all along…

***

I stood still while thinking whether I should use the window or the door to enter Amy's house. The door might be a better option because her mom will probably hear us sing and play.

I knock at the door. It's weird how Ms. Darren gives off horrible and terrifying vibes, while her own daughter gives heavenly atmosphere.

The door opens slowly and I saw a dark and tall figure standing there. She had a dark and long braid; she was wearing a navy blue dress and a gray apron.

I looked up at her, she had no expressions. "Hey, Ms. Darren. Is Amy home?"

"Can I help you?" her voice was deep and husky. What am I supposed to say now? The atmosphere felt dark and awkward.

"Mom, let her in" Amy shouts from her room. Her mom kept glaring me hard. She moved aside to make a way for me. I sprinted towards Amy's room as fast as possible.

I sat on her bed and asked "Now tell me, what about the guitar?" then I gasped "Don't tell me you stole your mom's money to buy me a new one!"

"No idiot, I don't have the guts to do it" then she sits on her knees on the floor, and tries to reach for something under the bed.

She takes out a dusty guitar, which had tons of things written on it. Oh wait, holy biscuits, it's my old guitar. "What the hell is this guitar doing under your bed?"

"Remember when you said that you lost your guitar," she says while dusting the guitar "You actually kept it under my bed for some reason, and I discovered it a month after we thought you lost it"

Okay I'm seriously so dumb. "I didn't return it to you because I saw you already got Mia's guitar, and so why would you want this old one back"

Dude, this guitar isn't old, it's my first ever guitar, my own. I have so many memories written on it. She hands me over the guitar and says "And guess what, my weird self wanted to learn to play a guitar all of a sudden, but I gave up too easily"

I look at the guitar and it feels so weird to hold it again. "Okay so, what song are we playing? Taylor Swift?"

"Sadly, no because, almost half the school will be playing Taylor. Let's go for something different" She has a point. Let's go for an unpopular, underrated song.

And for the next one hour, we spend time picking the best song, and trying to sing and play it. I swear we would make such an amazing duo. Ms. Darren also came to check on us, but actually she just wanted us to make a little less 'noise'.

We would be practicing the whole next week. We might win because of two reasons. One, me and Amy are one of the best musicians in our school. And two, others won't be taking it so seriously because they know that they just have to win or lose, but I'm fighting to stay or not...

Sage

Mom: We love our new apartment here!

I close my phone after I read that text. I'm frustrated now. Mom and dad decided to shift to Texas because things were really messed up back in Ohio. I am happy about it but they really didn't have to. But you know what, it doesn't really matter. After I'm done with the work, I'll visit them to see their apartment. They might need help with furniture.

I'm sitting in the restaurant all alone. It's closed now and it's getting late so I should just get out of here. Trev and Blair already left, I made them because sometimes being alone in a calm place at night is just so relaxing.

I leave the place, glancing at it one last time. I lock it turn around, bumping into someone. I look up at who it was, and what they were doing here so late. When I look up, my heart skipped a beat. I never realized how tall he was. I had a hard time removing my gaze from his blue sparkly eyes.

"Hey, are you guys closed already?" he asks. I just had my eyes wide open staring at him. Even though it was dark, his hair was shining. He was wearing a black hoodie. "Sage?"

"Oh yeah, um, well, yes we're closed but do you need something?" he puts his hands in the pocket and says "No but I was just curious what you're doing here all by yourself"

I smile "Because it's just so beautiful you know" I look up to point at the sky which was literally looking prettier than his oceanic eyes. "It feels good to sit alone and watch the moon for some reason" then he looks down and says "I saw you at Taco bell few days ago"

Wait, he recognized me? Then why did he ignore me? "I didn't come up to you because you told me to pretend like I don't know you in public, right?" He remembered my words? Oh my god! Wait, why am I so excited about it? Funny…

Does he remember the name I gave him? "What's you name?" I ask him with a straight face. He laughs at me and says "Clyder, it's originally it now"

Yes holy biscuits! I feel a sense of achievement for some reason. He starts walking with me. "You still remember the silly thing?" I giggled.

He looked down at me "I would never forgive myself if I forgot you. Even though I know nothing about you, you feel like, a personal diary"

Wow, I never thought about it that way "Okay sir, I'm you dear diary, what would you like to write today?" I joked. He smiled widely and said "Today I got chased by a bunch of dogs, they almost ripped my clothes apart" Okay that was so unnecessary.

"I have nothing special about me to express, why don't you go ahead"

I look up at him, then back at the path and said "Alright dear diary. I'm actually deciding on opening my own company. It would be selling skincare products. But I still don't know what to name it"

"That's so cool, actually. I know that, whatever you'll name it, it would be amazing because you're good at naming things, and even people" he laughs at his own joke. Whenever he mentions that I named him, it makes me flustered.

"Oh wait, I forgot," I started looking for something in the carry bag I had in my bag. "Here" I hand him over a box of three donuts.

"Donuts? Oh my god, thank you. Another fact about me, I'm in love with donuts" Can't believe that it's only our third time meeting and we're already so close and less awkward.

"I bought it for me and my cousins but I realized that I picked the wrong ones, these contain ingredients that they both are allergic to," I told him "You're not allergic to anything, right?"

"Luckily, nope"

"By the way, what were you doing at Taco bells? Trying to rob them?" I think that was a bad joke. He kept silent for a while, then says "I'm not actually broke though, I'm just unemployed. So I tried getting a job, just to keep myself busy. But they were already full and didn't need more workers"

One thing common about him and I is that we both live extraordinary lives. "Do you get weird dreams too?" I ask him out of curiosity, just in case we both have same problems. "No, I barely dream anything. I prefer reality over dreams"

He might be the only person whose life is weird but still likeable. I get a notification so I open my phone.

Mom: It's late now, so I'll come to the restaurant tomorrow. Go home now.

It's really not that late but it would be better if she visits the restaurant. Then I open the other chat.

Blair: Should I send Trevor to pick you up?

Me: No I'm alright.

"Where do you live though?" I ask him, still looking at my phone. He looks at me and says "Wanna visit for a while?"

I look at him and say "You have thirty minutes"

He grabs my wrist and takes an unexpected turn. "You really don't have to pull me, I can walk myself". "Alright"

He then says in a husky and deep voice "Sage," he wasn't looking at me "You know, you might be the first person to visit me"

I feel like I should be scared of him, but he's just so fine!

After a good ten minutes… I was at his house. It looked small but, it had *'home'* vibes.

When I entered it, I instantly fell in love. The only thing my eyes could notice was books. This house was more like a library. "You never mentioned that you loved books so much!"

"Take a seat, I only have fifteen minutes with you, as you said" he pulls a chair for me, but I was so busy with admiring the books. Then suddenly, he asks me something that made me want to scream.

"Sage, are you dating anyone?"

I wanted to answer him but my brain stopped functioning. So I gathered up my courage and said "N-no……and I don't think I'm planning to" oh my god, why did I say that?

He kept quite for a while after that. I found so many of those books that I have already read. I thought I was having one of the best moments of my life, until…

I saw a random red book. It looked very odd so I picked it up. Clyder was in the kitchen. I opened the book, and on the first page, there was something handwritten.

'I hope you're doing great :)'

What in the holy biscuits…

Isn't that… something I wrote years ago? I quickly look behind me to make sure Clyder isn't watching me. He was busy with whatever he was doing.

I remember that I wrote this note years ago when I visited a library with Amy. It's the same book, exact same book, exact same hand writing. The only difference about this book was that, it was empty that time but, *now it isn't.*

I secretly keep the book in my carry bag because it won't be very smart of me reading this book here. The only thought I had right now is that now, *something isn't right about this guy.*

"Hey, do you want me to drop you home?"

I flinch when he suddenly shows up. I knew that he could see the terror on my face. I was literally sweating. "Oh no, that's okay, I'll go myself"

He looks at me confused and asks "Are you okay?"

I kept walking slowly towards the door "Yeah I'm alright, I'm totally okay. What could possibly go wrong at this moment?" why am I trembling? "Sage, you're not okay. You're sweating. Are you not comfortable here?" he is so much concern about it "If that's the case then, I'll leave you alone" he looks down in disappointment. I feel so bad now. He actually made a close friend, and that close friend started feeling uncomfortable around him. "No, no Clyder. It's nothing like that, trust me" No Sage, no. Don't fall for him again. There is something wrong with him.

Even though he has the most prettiest eyes I've ever seen, or the cutest dimples ever, or the most attractive voice… he is really strange. He appeared in my dreams before I even met him and said weird stuff, then he has a bizarre story, and now he has a book that I found years ago back in Ohio which was empty, but now it's full?

"Alright, I trust you. It's really late anyways. And perhaps, thirty minutes is over I guess," he smiles "Bye and good night"

After I'm actually out, I run as far as I can from his house. I found a bus stop, so I sit right there. There were only few people around so I felt comfortable.

I take a long breath, and exhale. Then I open the book. When I flip the page, my eyes widen when I saw the author's name. It was……… *Sage Everitt.*

But I never wrote any book. What is my name doing here? My curiosity keeps rising and I cannot control myself. I flip the page to read the first line,

Sage Everitt took birth in Ohio, in a small house. She has a little sister named Evelyn Everitt……

Something isn't right here… I flip the pages more to read a random page,

Sage punched Chloe which caused her big trouble…

Then again turned leaving a very long gap,

She and her cousins went grocery shopping…

I was literally shaking. What the hell is this book? It's literally a book that recites each and every moment of my life. Being curious, I try to find that one page of my life…,

She stabbed her in the leg...

I immediately close the book back because I don't have the guts to read it. But how is this possible? Clyder can't be a stalker because this book is just too detailed. The book even talks about my dreams, and there is no way that a stalker would know my dreams. I open the pages when I met Clyder to see how the book addresses him before I named him. I open the pages when I saw him in the restaurant that day, and the wedding, then Taco bells, and then even of today, but... the book didn't mentioned him. It only mentions him when I see him in my dreams, as a *random guy*. But why? Why is he not mentioned?

Another strange thing about this book is that, whenever it talks about my bracelet, it refers it as *wristlet of cover*. Like,

Blair asked about the wristlet of cover...

Sage gets irritated because of the wristlet of cover...

He made fun of the wristlet of cover...

I turn to the page when I'm sitting here and reading this book. It still doesn't mention about Clyder, It says that I came out of the restaurant and instantly reached the bus stop. The pages after this were empty. They were yet to fill I guess.

There are so many questions in my mind. What is this book? Where did it come from? Why did Clyder have it? Who wrote it? How does this exist? What is this wristlet of cover?

But maybe I know exactly who can answer these questions. I immediately close the book and put it back to the bag. I take out my phone and text Blair.

Me: I'll be sleeping at my parent's apartment tonight. I'll see you guys tomorrow.

Few years ago

"Thank you so much Chloe, your performance was marvelous"

Chloe walks to the back stage after performing with her piano. "Oh my goodness Chloe! You were so fabulous on stage" said Carrie delightedly. She was literally being the most annoying person there. Chloe had the second performance. Amy and I had a lot of time to get ready.

I was just sitting in the corner, practicing my guitar and Amy was reviewing the lyrics. "Wow Sage, you're really gonna perform with that crappy old guitar? I wouldn't be caught dead with that thing" Chloe comes up to me with her venomous tongue.

I thought about arguing with her then and there, but it has no point. I just pretended that she wasn't even there. After she left, I turn towards Amy "Hey, are you sure about this? I've never performed in front of so many people. What if I mess up and we lose?"

She looks at me says "And what if you slay and win? Think about the positive side Sage." Then suddenly she stops as if she realized something.

She looks down to her feet and inhales deeply. Then she looks at me and says "Actually," her voice is very low "Is there any chance, we can, actually quit right now?"

Wait, just now she said that we might win, why does she wanna quit? "But you said we can win. Is there a problem?"

"Maybe. My throat doesn't feel well all of a sudden, I might crack up there…"

"Amy, that is a horrible lie, you were literally practicing your vocals a few minutes ago. What happened?" Amy's face was just full of tense and anxiety.

Then she says with a very serious face "You were right, you might mess up. We might lose. You heard Chloe play right? No one can beat her."

Now she's making me furious. Then I thundered bitterly "What the heck Amy? It was your idea to perform. You motivated me so much. And now you want me to quit? You want me to get expelled? Are you crazy? No, I won't quit without trying. And guess what, I believe I can win."

She rubs her face with her palms and says "What's the big deal of getting expelled? Thousands of kids drop out by their own choice. You're overreacting" I stare at her for a few seconds. This is unbelievable. I know that getting expelled isn't a huge deal but, she doesn't know that I'll move far away from her if I get expelled. I know that that's normal too but I wouldn't be able to contact Amy again because of Ms. Darren. This case very different from normal.

"Amy," I try to stay calm "I am not one of those thousands of kids. And now I don't want to argue about anything." She has lost her mind.

We keep quite for a few minutes. Amy breaks the silence "I'm sorry" I don't want her apology, she has lost her brain and that's it.

Amy walks away somewhere. I don't know why she's acting so damn weird. She isn't going to the washroom, where is she going? There is something off about her today.

I decided to follow her. It feels hella odd to follow Amy secretly to see what's up with her. The whole school was empty because everyone was in the auditorium. Only a few kids were roaming around. She kept walking and walking.

Then suddenly she takes a turn, where we never went. This might be the first time for me to see this side of the school.

Now I can't see or hear anyone else except Amy. I could only hear her footsteps in the whole hallway. I tried walking as quietly as I can. But because of that, I lost her.

"Where did she go?" I mumbled to myself. I start looking around, and I find a door open. There was no one around and that door was open randomly. That means that Amy went inside.

It was a store room. Why would she go inside? I knew something was off with her. I know it isn't really smart of me going inside to see what she's up to, but I cannot control myself.

So I start walking towards the door. My footsteps were very clearly audible. I couldn't hear Amy anymore. All I heard were my footsteps, and the cold breeze. The lights were dim. And the store room was dark.

I stepped inside. It was dark but I could still see the room. I couldn't see Amy though. "Amy?" I whispered. But there was no response.

So I turned around to leave but, as I was about to step out, someone shut the door on me. I flinched because of the sudden movement. The next second, I realized that someone was trying to sabotage me. I gasped and tried to push the door open. The person who was trying to shut me inside and I, both were applying the same strength. I screamed "Who the hell are you?!"

I was scared that I'll be trapped in here and I wouldn't be able to perform. My heart was pounding hard. I've only seen these types of scenarios in movies. I am not aware of what I'm doing, I just pushing hard mindlessly. I'm scared, I'm really scared. There was no use of screaming because I knew no one could hear me. I didn't even have my phone.

Then I applied all of my strength to push the door, and that person fell down. I was about to run away so hard without even caring who the person was because I was so frightened. But just as I came out and saw the person, my heart sank. My whole body got heated up. I felt like I was carrying a huge, heavy rock and I can be crushed by it anytime. I just stared at the person very hard. I felt like I couldn't move my body anymore, as if it was broken. I really am broken…

"A…Amy?"

She stood up slowly. I couldn't help myself but just don't move. It was like I was divided in three different humans. One who wanted to yell at her, one who wanted to ask her what the hell is happening, and one who wanted to just runaway from her.

Her hands were on her neck, it was hurt I suppose. But the only emotion I had that moment was, uncertainty.

I start walking towards her slowly, and before I know it, she pushed me. *She pushed me harsh.* But this time I pulled in her in the room with me.

She screamed "LET ME GO" I yelled back at her "AS IF" It was dark inside and we both were on the ground. I saw her trying to find something on the floor.

The next moment, I felt intense pain on one of my legs. My grip on Amy's hand loosen. I placed my hand to touch and see what hurts me. It felt like a knife.

She stabbed me.

Amy stands up but doesn't leave, she was just looking at me. Right now I had millions of things and millions of questions, but the only thing that came out of my mouth was "W…why did you s…stab me? Amy?" I could barely speak anything properly.

"Don't ask me Sage, please. Don't…" she says in a faint voice "Just remember that, no one has ever mattered to me, but you do, just remember that. And trust me, I never wanted to do this"

I have no clue what to speak. A person just tried to lock me in a dark room and also stabbed me, and now saying that I matter to them the most and telling me to trust them?

"Amy, YOU STABBED ME"

"I KNOW! I have a reason… I swear…" she falls to her knees and starts crying. I was still on the floor because I cannot bear the pain. My leg was bleeding. A goddamn knife was stabbed in my leg and I'm bleeding so much, but still, all I could see is Amy.

Amy on her knees crying and telling me that she never wanted to do this. But Amy who tried to lock me in alone, and is the cause of my bleeding leg.

"I am not doing this intentionally. I am forced to do this." She gulps "Answer me, what would you choose? Me, or a bright future with all your dreams?"

I keep quite because I don't know why she's asking this. And if I think about it maturely, we need to build our future first, but that doesn't come with the cost of losing your best friend. "Sage, I am doing this because of my mom and Chloe" she cries hard.

It wouldn't matter to me if it was someone else. If it was Evelyn, Emma, Chloe or anyone else, I would just stand up and punch them and then just leave them here as if nothing happened. But the case is here that, it's Amy who did this to me.

"My mom always threatens me that, if I get expelled or suspended because of any mischief, she will never help me with my law school or anything in the future. And Chloe threatened me. She said that if you win, she will get me expelled instead of you. I know that I should have told you about it but, it was too late to do anything and I wanted to end it the simple way. And mom hates you Sage. The only way for me to build my future and become a lawyer, was for you to hate me. I am a very weak and hopeless person who's just scared to live a miserable life"

My whole world shattered before my eyes. I could feel myself burning "THAT'S NOT A CONVINCING REASON, AMY. You destroyed our years of friendship. And you believe that you will be glad with your future, *without me?*"

"I had no choice. It was hard breaking us casually because it was impossible"

That's true, it would break us within. But if hatred is formed, the hate would automatically build barriers. It's like I'm in a prison, and there's no way to escape.

"There was nothing else that could make you hate me. Even if I spoke rubbish of your family, you would believe that something miserable has happened to me. Even if I told Mr. Ben directly, you wouldn't believe that I did it and blame it on Chloe"

That's true too. I always find excuses to accept her.

"But what I did today, will truly make you hate me, even if I tried apologizing hard, Trust me Sage, I love you but, I'm forced…"

Hearing the truth felt like I had been doused in ice cold water. Her words said that *I'm sorry, I love you and I always will. It doesn't matter if you hate me…* but actions speak louder than words and they said that *I do very bad things, and I do them well.*

I wanted to tell her that she didn't do anything wrong so there's nothing to apologize for, but that's not right. "Do you even know what you caused?"

She looks up at me, ashamed. "I didn't want to drop out because it will affect me to move out of the country, away from you" She widens her eyes in disbelief. I could tell that she had no words to my statement.

I am not angry because she stabbed me or tried to sabotage me. I am angry because she lied all those years saying that *nothing could cause us to break.* She lied that she loved me because she's just self-seeking.

"I never wanted us to end up like this Sage…"

"There is no *'us'*, there never was" I didn't even realized that I was crying. She sobs and says "It wasn't suppose to go this far, I swear"

"YOU'RE JUST BEING SELFISH, AMY. This is what you wanted, right? For me to hate you? I FREAKING HATE YOU! YOU ARE JUST LIKE YOUR MOM!"

She stands up slowly, crying harder than ever. "SAGE! Please I can't take this anymore……"

"Oh yes you have to, because this is what YOU wanted. YOU'RE A SOCIOPATH!!"

She takes a long breathe, runs here fingers through her hair and says "I promise you that, I'll come back. Because you are my only best friend"

"NO DON'T COME BACK. Right now you're getting me out of here, and getting lost from my sight."

She runs away, locking the door behind her and leaving me in alone. "AMY!" I tried standing up but I totally forgot that… *my best friend stabbed me in the leg.*

I fell back on the ground with greater pain than before. I couldn't do anything so I just lie down and cry. I wanted to scream so loudly but I didn't have the energy to do it.

What just happened here?

The last ten minutes escalated so fast. From arguing to confusion, from confusion to terror, from terror to pain, from pain to betrayal and from betrayal to hatred.

A part of me still refuses to believe that this happened. This can't happened. Did Amy and I just end our friendship like this? This just doesn't sit right.

Suddenly Chloe's words start to build in my head.

I am just a human, I feel pain, I trip and fall, I cry, I talk to myself because only I know what I go through. I am just a human, I get puzzled, I mess up, I feel devastated, voices in my head humiliate me.

Is this one of my weird dreams? Maybe I'm dreaming too hard. No, I should stop making excuses because, I never dream with anyone that I see in real life. This is reality, the truth, the fate, the life.

I pick up a bucket nearby and throw at the door. Then I start to throw more things. And I don't know if that would help. I sit down, and hug my knees. At this point, I have no idea how I'm going to get out.

If it wasn't Amy who did this to me, she would be the one to save me and stab the person who did this. But here, she is the person who stabbed me. Maybe I would love to drop out now and go away from here.

I thought I always related to her, but I'm pretty sure I wouldn't do this to her. Actually, I won't do this to anyone, not even Chloe. Leaving someone alone in a dark room, knowing that they are bleeding severely… this just isn't my thing.

Just as I thought, someone opens the door.

She looks at me and gasps "Oh my god Sage, what happened here?" she quickly gets to her knees.

"Evelyn…" I hug her very tight. This is the first time we are hugging each other. It might be a little awkward for her but, I need it.

She rubs my back "What's going on?"

I tell her every bit of what happened here. It felt like I'm telling Amy about all my problems, but the case here is different. Here, she is the problem.

I could see Evelyn hiding her tears. "I knew it" she says in a stone-hard voice "Sage, she didn't deserve you anyways"

"Lyn, that's the most pointless and common thing anyone would say right now" I wipe my tears and fix my hair "Do you think Amy is not guilty. I mean, she said she's forced and I feel like I understand"

Her face suddenly turns jaded "Stop making the excuses Sage. If she really loved you, she would never put herself in a position to lose you"

Maybe that's right. Actually, that really is right. Now that I think about it, Amy was an amazing friend, a comforting, soft and motivating friend. But I always tried to hide her toxic side. I made excuses and made her seem like she was perfect. But she wasn't.

At this point, I want to leave this city and this very memory behind. If I could, I would literally just walk up to Mr. Ben myself, and tell him that I smacked his daughter on the face because she was being an asshole.

After this day, there is no way she would have the courage to walk up to me. Just a few days more until the session ends.

Bye Ohio, Bye Amy.

Usually it takes me so much time to process the sudden shocking or depressed moments. But I'm not only shocked this time. I'm heart-broken. I'm sick. I feel the sort of pain I've never felt before.

Even though I said that I wanna leave the city and forget everything that happened today, I never really meant it. Whatever happened, seems so fake and unrealistic. I am just saying what I feel, or at least trying to. She didn't say goodbye, and a part of me believes that means she's coming back.

You were the first person I ever showed my heart to, and you're the reason no one will see it again.

Sage

I knock really hard. I didn't meant to be loud but it just came out naturally, or maybe accidently. No one was opening the door so I knock again, and I instantaneously heard the door unlock.

I keep my hand on my forehead and move my hair back. I realized that I was still sweating and I was breathing noisily. The door opened.

"Sage!" she hugs me with an extensive smile "What are you doing here? Didn't you get my message?"

"I did mom," I enter inside and keep the carry bag on the table and took a seat on the couch "I wanted to talk about something"

She sits down slowly, looking concern. "Nice apartment though. When do you plan to buy new furniture?"

"Oh there's no rush. We just have this couch and table, and a mattress in the other room"

The place isn't too big nor too small. It's just perfect, or at least just the way they like it. I look around the house. It is all white in color. It kind of brings me joy that they're here in Texas now. Dad comes out of the washroom and smiles widely when he sees me. He looked really dull and ill. "Dad, are you sick?"

He takes a seat beside me. He was coughing. "Oh, no honey I'm okay. Just a little fever you know" he pours me a glass of water kept on the table and hands it to me "It's so late, is there a problem?"

I take the glass and put it back to the table without drinking. I don't want to ask them questions right now. Dad is sick and they both are so happy to see me after so long. I don't wanna ruin the moment by asking creepy questions.

To be honest, I feel like I'm in a fantasy. Like you know, *magic*. I sound so childish while saying it but like, isn't this like a magical fantasy story? It's like, I'm from another world.

A girl with a bracelet on which can never be removed, and she gets creepy and weird dreams which includes unrealistic people, but she meets a boy from her dreams in real life, and he has a book which contains the telling of her whole damn life.

Yeah, that's definitely not normal. But I don't even how to start this thing. What do I ask them first?

I didn't even notice that mom went to the kitchen. "Are you hungry?"

"Mom, do you even have supplies to make something? Ya'll just moved in"

"At least a sandwich I guess"

I try to smile to make the atmosphere a little relaxing. Then dad said "How's your restaurant going? And how's our man Trevor?"

"He's alright. And our restaurant is going blast. It's doing so good, but it's so unexpectedly excellent and I just can't believe it" my mood just upgraded so quick. But right now, I don't want to be happy, I wanna seriously talk about what I came here for.

"Mom,"

"Yeah what is it"

I pat a seat beside me and motion her to sit "Come here" she comes and sits casually. I stood up and sat on a chair while they both sit on the couch in front of me. They both are silent and baffled.

"Mom, don't you think I'm old enough to understand," I lift my wrist and point at my bracelet "what is it?"

Dad rests his head on the couch. Mom sighs and says bitterly "For the thousandth time, it's nothing serious, and never mind it"

"So you mean I'll live my whole life with this thing on without knowing its purpose?" I stand up "It costs nothing to tell me what's on my wrist. It's my body and I don't even know what's on it? I have the right to know what this thing is"

"Just tell her, it's not like she's gonna escape" dad said and just walks back to the bedroom, coughing. My eyes follow his walking figure, and when he's gone, I look back at mom expecting a reply. She nods and says "Alright, sit down"

I do as she says. Then looks deep in my soul and asks "Why did you suddenly get curious about it after so many years?"

I move my gaze down at the table. Then I reach out for my bag and I take out the book. Without a word, I give the book to her.

She looks at the book for a few seconds. Before opening the book, she looks at me, then drops her eyes back to the book. She flips the pages pretty fast and says "There's literally nothing"

What kind of silly crap is this? I snatch the book from her and open it. I widen my eyes when I again see…nothing. How? Are my eyes playing tricks on me? I close my eyes aggressively and open it again, but there was still nothing. Not even my handwritten note.

"Are you going crazy, Sage?" Am I going crazy? Maybe I am going crazy. No I believe I'm not going crazy. "No it's impossible"

"You going crazy isn't impossible"

"No, I mean, the book. It was full before I came here. It was a crazy book with the telling of my life" Mom looks at me with a puzzled face "Telling of your life? Sage, you need to sleep because you really are going crazy"

I groan because I'm seriously annoyed. "This isn't right. This book had so many things written like about Lyn, Blair, Trevor and other many people, it was so crazy with weird things written like my dreams and a sort of wristlet of cover thingy and…"

"Wait what" she interrupts me.

I knew it. I said the wristlet of cover on purpose, to see her reaction. She was trying to hide her reaction but I knew the case. I place the book down and cross my arms "Mom, what is this bracelet, or should I say, *wristlet of cover"* the fun part here is that I just saw her gulp. I ain't leaving this place without all my answers.

"I guess you're right, maybe I should spit it out" "Obviously"

"You might have heard the common saying '*When we all fall asleep, where do we go?'"*

I'm not sure if I've ever heard the saying but I've heard a song with the same name. Billie Eilish you know. "Yeah, I did. What does it has to do anything with this bracelet?"

"Because the bracelet is related to the peculiar dreams you get"

I knew it, I always knew it. *Oh god, oh god, Oh God....* It feels creepy just the way it's unwrapping.

"Sage, look, you…" just as she was saying, a sound interrupted her. It was a sound of glass breaking. And it came from the bedroom.

Oh no, dad.

Just as me and mom realized, we ran to the bedroom, to find dad on the ground. "Oh my god!" mom screamed. I stood they're horrified. Mom got down to her knees and tried to wake him up. She was already crying. What do I do?

I started panicking. I had no clue what should I do, it happened so suddenly. I quickly start looking for my phone in my bag but couldn't find it because my hands were shaking. I was mumbling stuff like "Oh god please no, no, no, no"

I quickly find it and dial a number. "Sage, please be quick" mom was sobbing. I was frightened so bad and losing my temper. He picked up the call.

"Yeah?" he said in a dull voice. "T…Trevor, we need h…help" I could hear him getting alarmed "Sage, what happened? Are you okay? Why are you crying?"

"Trev, I'm sending you the address of my parent's new apartment. Please be quick, we need to go to the hospital"

"Don't worry, I'm on my way"

I quickly hang up and text him the address. Dad was still on the ground. I am scared, *really scared.* I bring a glass of water and sprinkle it on his face. He wasn't waking up. He was still breathing though. I could only hear mom crying and my heavy breathing, when I also become conscious that it was raining outside.

"Dad?" I said in a faint voice. I don't even know the logic behind it.

This isn't right. None of it.

Within a few minutes, Trevor arrives at our floor. Trevor lifts him by placing his arms behind our neck. The way from here to the car was exhausting. "Mrs. Everitt, we'll take him to the hospital…" "No! I'm coming"

"Trevor, let her, please". He nods. "It's raining"

There wasn't too much traffic luckily. I knew dad was sick but I didn't know he was *this* sick. He is old now and he needs to take care of himself. In point of fact, I am so damn appreciative that they're in the same city now. I have no clue how mom would have handled this back in Ohio. Sometimes I fear that this maybe has happened before but they didn't inform me about it.

We reached the hospital and the doctors immediately started to check. I tried to calm mom down because she was in such a bad state after crying. Trevor handed us a bottle of water and told me to settle down. Worrying about mom and dad, I didn't realized how badly I was panicking and shivering in trepidation.

After a couple of minutes, mom was finally serene, and I was free of apprehension. We were sitting outside the room and Trevor was roaming around with his arms crossed. The doctor came out.

"Everything is okay" as soon as we heard it, we left out a big sigh of relief. "He was just stressed and ill, and he is old now so they need to take extra care of himself" I knew it. But I won't say *I told him so.* Because I know that there is a difference between saying and doing.

Advising someone to take more care of themselves is easy, but it isn't easy for each one of us to do so. My dad always believes that he is super healthy and full of stamina all the time. He used to say "An illness is nothing to me, it doesn't effect me" but he doesn't understand that it effects us instead. He will understand over time that he is old now, and every person suffers it. There are many ways to enjoy life without being strenuous or stressful.

Should I be thankful to Clyder? I mean, if he didn't show up in front of the restaurant, he wouldn't have invited me, and then I wouldn't have found the book and have urge to ask mom all of the crap.

We were lucky, I guess.

"Can I meet him?" mom asks the doctor and he nods. She rushes to the room. Then suddenly Trevor's phone started ringing. He looks at his phone, then looks at me and says "It's Blair. I'll tell her everything is fine. Will you spend the night here?"

"Yeah, you can go. I guess we will be leaving tomorrow morning. We'll catch an Uber to home"

He nods and picks up the call. I enter the room to meet dad.

Sage

"I'm so screwed" said Blair. "At least Trev didn't see you trip"

The restaurant was so quite. Not the *bad* quite. It was calm and relaxing, just like lunchtime should be. Well, Blair's morning didn't go as good as I'm describing it. She accidently tripped and broke a plate.

Just one plate.

Her face tells that she's kind of mortified. Trevor has gone out to meet his doctor. Not just any doctor.

A doctor that he's dating.

We both requested him to bring her here today for lunch. But I doubt it because I think she'll be busy. She's a doctor, after all.

"I really feel bad for her" she says, resting her chin in her palms "She'll get so annoyed by Trevor's lame jokes"

"Maybe he acts different around her?" that sounded more like a question than a statement. Because I'm confused by my own words.

Does he act different?

"Maybe, I don't know about that" then she groans "Where is Trev! I'm starving!" just as she said that, Trevor enters the place. But it was just him, alone. He didn't bring his girl. "Her schedule was tight" he says as he puts a paper bag on the slab. "What's this?"

"She sent lunch for us. Its spaghetti". Okay, she's already my favorite.

Me and Blair literally took out the box in less than ten seconds.

"Ah! Thank you, I was so damn hungry" she opens the box "Is she making spaghetti in the hospital?"

"No dimwit, she was at her house. She made extra for us and was about to come here. But she got an emergency so she just gave it to me"

We start walking towards our office because we ain't eating in front of the customers. Today is going to be a busy day, I just feel it.

We already started eating and let me tell, this might be the best spaghetti I've ever had. Trevor's phone started ringing "Give me a minute" he was about to leave but Blair pulled him back to sit "Is it her?". He didn't respond to that and just rolled his eyes. "Pick it up here"

"No"

"Yes"

"No way"

"Yes way"

So Blair just snatched his phone and picked up the call. Trev didn't even snatch it back. "Alright, I guess ya'll can have some chit chats"

"Hey!" Blair says ecstatically on the phone "I'm Blair, Trevor's sister you know. Before you say anything, I want to tell you that you are an amazing cook" that was so true. I could hear laughing from the other side. And then I assume she said thank you. I couldn't hear her properly but her voice sounded so *doctor-ey*. That's not even a word but like, I mean she sounded like a doctor which she really is. I wonder how pretty she is.

The doctor was talking more, about Trevor I guess. But Blair wasn't smiling anymore. She looked a little off all of a sudden. "Blair, I wanna talk too" I raise my hand to grab the phone but then she backs away a few steps.

"Well, the call disconnected. I guess she got busy again" she says and hands over the phone to Trevor. "She called just to know how the food was. And she said that she would love to meet us very soon"

I wish I was as busy as she is. I love being distracted by work. Especially when I want to forget something. I want to forget what happened last night. *Clyder. Book. Wristlet of cover. Dad.*

After a few minutes when we were done eating, Trevor and Blair headed out to work. I took out the book to see if it's still blank. I brought this book in case I see Clyder again so I can confront him. I don't want to visit his house because his neighbors might find it weird that a girl is visiting a house that no one else ever visited except the owner. I open the book, and yes, it wasn't blank. It's again printed. There is something magical going on in my life. I sound so dim-witted while is say it, but it might be a fact.

The book was only printed till when dad fainted. I guess it's slow?

I open my phone to see the texts. I haven't checked my phone after I called Trevor last night. I had so many notifications. Most of them were useless emails and YouTube notifications. I opened to see the texts. There was a text Blair sent me last night when I was in hospital, but I'm seeing it now

Blair: I hope you're alright.

I really hope I was, but all I am, is confused. Then there was a text from mom that was sent ten minutes ago

Mom: Let's talk. Are you busy today?

I am, but I want to clear everything up. I want to know about what I'm living with. I thought mom will take dad's illness as an excuse to ignore my questions. But I guess she thought a lot about it. I really didn't want to pressure her but, it is what it is. I look forward to not being selfish regarding it.

***

"Are you feeling any better?" I ask him as I take a seat beside him lying on the bed. "Ugh, I'm always better. This is nothing. I will be running and jumping after a few days" I love to hear his positivity "dad, you know that you should focus on recovery other than focusing on what to do after recovery"

Mom brings in his medicine "Yes, tell him Sage. He still thinks he is a youngster" I know, what can I expect from him.

"Hash tag forever young"

That made me laugh a lot. But it's time for me to talk about why I'm here. Mom and I come out of the room because we ain't stressing dad out.

"When we all fall asleep, where do we go?" I say once I sit down on the couch and mom sitting in front of me "This wristlet is linked with my mind? That's funny, mom"

"It isn't funny. And Sage, I promise that whatever I'm going to say, is nothing but truth. It would be bitter and terrifying, but you know it won't change anything" it doesn't sound good. She takes in a very long breathe as if she's about to talk very long nonstop. Which I assume she will…

"I don't know how to start this. If I'm straight forward, I might sound like an idiot"

"Just be clear-cut"

"You're not from earth" what kind of prank is this. I don't give a reaction because that was a stupid joke "I sounded stupid, didn't I?"

"Totally"

"Okay, let me be not so basic. Sage, our life consists of two world. Two worlds that can never meet"

That sounds funny. But not a joke. She's serious. Seriously serious. What the heck? There is literally no logic in this crap. "When we all fall asleep, we dream. We dream about what happened in our life. We dream about our family and friends. Can you answer, what you dream about?"

I know what type of answer she's expecting from me "Dreams which consists of people that I've never seen in real life" I said that as if I started to realize something. "Sage, you are here, in this world, but only *partially*"

What in the actual holy biscuits?

"That bracelet, wristlet of cover, is a bracelet for protection. To protect you from leaving the world so that you won't enter the other world"

"What? Wait, you mean, I am suppose to live in the other world? But you guys are preventing from it to happen?" I would have never believed her but, the bracelet, the book and Clyder, all of these aren't normal. She might have a point.

"Let me make this clear. Yes, you are supposed to live in the other world. But accidently, you took birth here and I didn't wanted to give you up, so we got this bracelet to prevent it to happen. And so you lived here normally. But when you are dreaming at night, you enter that world"

That might be true, because when I dreamed about those people calling me Valerie, Clyder said that I'm not aware. *That means I wasn't aware that I was dreaming.*

"When you are awake here, as Sage Everitt, your other half if living as another human being in that world" She might be talking about Valeria.

Oh my goodness…

"You are officially Sage Everitt because you remember only the memories of this world, and live in that world when asleep. The other half is nothing, she remembers nothing, just lives in place of you in that world when you're awaken"

"Why me? Why just me?"

"It's not only you. There are many people who are accidently born here instead of there. But only a few are lucky enough to get that wristlet."

There is literally something wrong. This is weird. I feel strange, horrified, shock, lost, but for time ever… I'm not confused.

"Okay, I get it" but actually I don't. *I'm not from this world?* How come? This feels, so damn crazy. I've never felt this sort of pain. This was such a big thing and, mom didn't tell me anything? All these years? This is unbelievable. I was right, it is magical. I live in a fantasy. *Wow.*

I can't believe that not everyone knows this. This is insane, and exciting, and horrifying.

"But what does this has a connection with the book?"

"Everything that you find extraordinary or out of this world, like that book you're talking about… all of these are the message from the other world. They aren't real, they're you're imagination. Only you can see them. See, you found that book, and you started questioning everything. And that made you know everything"

All of these make so much sense now. All of it. Everything is so much clear now. But I'm not relieved. I feel heavy. So much heavy. I want to cry out loud so bad, but I was already tearing up. I wiped away the tears because I have to ask this really important thing "Is it possible that a person from that world enter this world without the wristlet of cover?"

"No, absolutely not"

Oh, My, God. Does that mean that… *Clyder is no one?* He is just a message? *Just an imagination?* No wonder he had no name. No wonder Trev couldn't see his face the first time we met. He is from the other world…

I could cry right now. All the sweet and random moments we created together, I just imagined those? None of it was real?

I want to run away from here and just sob. But there is just one last and final question that is left to ask "Mom, you said that only a few are lucky enough to get this wristlet. Where did you get it?"

"My grandmother gave it to me. She said that, her grandmother gave it to her. It has been just passing around."

She was about to say more but she stopped. "And?" I asked. She just looked at me, then down at her legs. "Mom?" I knew what she was hiding "What was the cost?" no one can save a life for free. There must be a cost. Obviously.

She hesitated to speak. I stared intensely at her. I'm not leaving without answers. "The cost was…… for you to have no siblings" I knew where this was going. My heart started pounding "That's why I had to keep you and Lyn away from each other" she wasn't making any eye contact with me. I felt so weighty. It was like I was penetrating deep in the ground. This wasn't supposed to happen so quickly. Now I wish I never questioned it, and let it be the way it is.

I stood up aggressively "Mom, you kept my sister away from me my whole life, without telling me why. I hated her so much! If once, only once you told me the reason, maybe I would have treated her better" I was full of rage and didn't know what crap I was spitting "You kept her away from all of us mom. That's the reason you don't know what she's going through. That's the reason you don't know she has Dyspraxia. You're the damn reason that she felt adopted and abandoned!" and just like that, I stormed out of the house without any reactions or words of hers.

Sage

I was sitting in the middle of my messy room. The pillows were on the floor, because I threw them. The pages of few note books were ripped, because I rip them. I was in my pajamas, and the clothes were on my bed. The closet was open wide. There were twenty missed calls from mom.

After I left my mom's apartment, I totally engaged myself in the restaurant. I kept my mind distracted the whole day. I was staring at the ceiling fan. I am devastated. Today was really exhausting. The spaghetti was the only good part of the day.

Now I'm so, I don't know. I feel lost. I wonder if mom is lying. But there's no way because the book, it's not ordinary. Should I tell Blair?

She is like my own sister. I never hide anything from her, and she says the same too but I'm not sure. After Amy left me, I never got attached to anyone. It was like, I totally changed. If Amy met me today, she would definitely notice the extreme changes. I got into depression for a few months. It got so bad that, even my new teachers thought I was an Emo.

I didn't notice but my actions were rude. My classmates told me how mean I was. I didn't realize how depressed I was until I started journaling my thoughts and noticed how much I cried, every single day. I thought I needed to talk to Lyn, but then she was even far from us. And for the first time, I missed her.

Blair only visited us in Columbus once in two to three years. But while she did, her, Amy and I were like the best trio ever. Blair and I weren't so close back then, when everything changed.

She was the only person I talked to back then, *over texts*. I told her about Amy. I never met anyone more comforting than her. We were so young. And as I said that I never got attached to anyone after Amy, I was wrong. It was her I got attached to.

I want to tell her about today, but this might be the only topic where she would think I lost my mind. Fair enough. Even I would laugh if someone told me that they're not from this world.

What hurts me the most is that, Clyder isn't real. Why? That 'why' isn't a question for "why is Clyder not real?". It's a question for "why do I care?"

Why do I care about whether he is real or just an imagination? When did I start to get so close to him? It's only been a few months. But, perhaps, I should have recognized his lies.

He said he was poor and a homeless type of guy at the wedding, but all of a sudden he admits that he isn't broke. *And* he owns a whole damn library? Yeah…no.

I sit down and pull a rubber band out of my wrist. I made a high bun because my hair is annoying the heck out of me. Then I hear a sound. Sound of pages turning. It was like someone just flipped through all the pages of a book. I look around on the bed to see what's making the sound.

The book. The red book. It was making the sound. I reached out for it. I guess it makes this sound when there is a change?

I flip through the pages but there was no change. Still on the same spot of dad fainting. I guess I was wrong. I throw the book on the edge of the bed. I was about to stand up to get dinner, but then I noticed a folded sheet peeking out of the book. I slowly get more comfortable on the bed and pull the book towards me. I take out the paper and open it. I guess that's the thing making the sound.

It contained handwritten stuff. But, the handwriting is so damn pretty. It was like a letter. I sit comfortably and start reading it.

Dear Sage,

I hope your okay, which I assume your not. First of all, I'm sorry. Second of all, I'm really sorry. I don't want to say this but, I told you. I already told you not to come up to me the day you were dreaming about me. That was the first time you talked to me while dreaming. That was the first time you saw me in your dreams. That was the first time I talked to Sage Everitt, and not Valerie.

People fall in love with celebrities, anime characters, fictional characters……but I guess you fell for your own imagination. What hurts the most is that I can't even meet you, and you don't even know me. What hurts even more is that, I don't want Valerie, I want you.

All of this might be a little confusing for you, so let's talk in a language that you'll understand. First of all, thank you. Second of all, I can't thank you enough.

You know, I might be just an imagination here with you, but it hurts so bad. Hurts to be nameless. Hurts to be alone. Hurts to be invisible to the world. You saved me, Sage.

You talk to me, only you. And when you're the only person who knows me, and the person I know, you might be just, the most incredible person to me. Thank you, it's hard to explain what it feels like to be visible to someone when no one knows you.

You named me Sage. I don't know about you, but you're the only one I ever think about. Come back to this world Sage, please. Stop living in your nightmares as if it's your reality. The place you think is your dream, is actually your life. It's heavenly here. It's more peaceful and less confusing. Come back.

Yours,

Clyder

I crumble up the paper and throw it to the corner of the room. I bury my face into my pillow, my breathe slowly escaping my lungs. I felt a scream clawing and tugging at my throat, begging to be let out. But all I could let out was the faintest, tiniest, quietest scream. Not feeling satisfied, I continue to silently sob, as my shaky body, slowly curled up into a little ball.

I remember when I used to doubt my existence, I guess I was right.

Sage

"It's good right?" Blair asks me while looking around the building. "We can paint it all white, with bright lights. Or we can get light pastel colors. It should have like, you know, clean vibes"

She was literally trying her best to describe her ideas and I totally get it. We just got this place for my store. We're planning on how it would look. "This needs cleaning though"

She groans and says "I'm so hungry!"

"Blair, you're always hungry" well so am I. Lunch time already past one or two hours ago and we didn't eat anything. Trevor is at the restaurant. I take a seat on a dusted chair after placing a cloth on it. "That might be broken" Blair nods her head towards the chair.

I open my phone to call Trevor and tell him that we love the place, but he already texted me.

Trevor: Don't call me, it's a rush here and I'll be busy. And your so called sister-in-law is free today so I gave her the address of that place, she will be there in a while.

I stand up in excitement "She's coming!" Blair spits out the water she was drinking "Who's coming?"

"Her!!"

"Sage, I can't possibly understand who *'her'* is" I roll my eyes "Her!

The girl Trevor is dating" as I said this, I pictured Blair's face lighting up and her clapping in excitement. But her reaction was almost opposite. Her face turned as if she saw a ghost. Then she looks down and crosses her arms. "Blair, what's up?"

She looks up at me and moves her head "No it's nothing. I guess I'm just too exhausted to meet her right now" I sigh and say "I know. Alright, we'll just have a quick introduction and plan a dinner night for later. I believe she can understand" Blair face looked like she still wasn't really satisfied with my plan. But we couldn't plan anything else because a car was honking outside, that means she arrived!

I looked at Blair and smiled widely. I moved to go outside but Blair held my arm "Wait. You stay here, I'll bring her inside"

"Why do you wanna bring her inside? There's nothing to show her here" but she just walked away to her. There's definitely something off with her. Or maybe with *them.*

I quickly walk towards the door and peek to see what's going on. And when I saw the person who was sitting in the car, talking to Blair, I felt like my heart wanted to come out the throat. I felt shivers down body and my heart was thumping loud and fast. I knew she would return, but I didn't know that she would return like this.

I promise you that, I'll come back. Because you are my only best friend.

Right now I can't believe my eyes. But why is she so happy right now? Why is Amy smiling? Is it funny to her that she is dating my brother? Well it isn't. Why is Blair not punching her in the face? Why are they having a casual conversation? I wanted to walk up there and slap her hard, but she just drove away after waving a bye to Blair. I don't really think she is dating Trevor, I just feel it. I go back inside and wait for Blair.

She slowly walks inside and says looking at me "You saw her, didn't you" I don't answer because I'm scared I might lose my mind. I'll either yell at her, or cry.

Breathe in, breathe out.

"Why was she here?" I ask very calmly. She sighs and says "Sage, we can sort this out. Just in case you're wondering, she isn't dating Trev"

I knew it, that couldn't happen, I just know it. But I don't show my relief and I keep a straight face "Then why was she here Blair?" my voice sounded stone-hard. Before she could reply me, Amy comes in. She looks at both of us and hands Blair a carry bag "I forgot to give it to you. I made spaghetti again, since ya'll loved it last time"

Again? She made spaghetti, *again?* That means she really is dating Trevor. And that also means that Blair is trying to lie to me. She looks as me with a smile "You must be Sage, right?"

I shouldn't have, but I yell at her "What do you mean by 'I must be Sage'? Stop acting like an idiot" I regret it. I shouldn't have yelled at her so suddenly. It's been so many years. But she really is acting like a numb head.

She looks at me worryingly "Why? I'm sorry if I offended you in any way but, I'm pretty sure you really are Sage, aren't you?" I look at Blair confused. It was like, Blair knew all the answers but she wasn't even trying to explain.

I guess Amy is just being sarcastic.

"Why are you here?" I ask Amy as arrogantly. It feels so weird to have her in front of me right now. I'm *actually* talking to Amy. She hasn't really changed, it's just that she looks prettier. Trevor didn't really know Amy as my best friend back then, that's why they ended up dating. Or else if he knew what this girl can do for herself, he would never.

"You're not actually dating Trevor because you love him, right? You're using him to get to me. You're freaking using my brother to get closer to me." I was moving forward to her, backing her off. Blair holds my shoulder "Sage, stop"

I remove it and point at Amy "Get out of his life before I stab you like you did" I felt my tone get louder. If I said one more sentence, that would yelling loud.

I just turn around and wait for her to leave. And I finally turn around when I heard her footsteps leaving.

"That was vulgar, Sage" Blair hissed "You hurt her"

"So did she, you don't realize? I was just doing fine, really, and then she's trying to come back to my life like she never knew me before"

"Being like that doesn't make you any different than her" she places her hands behind her neck and looks up. I felt my eyes burning and tearing up. I could picture myself with a red face "Blair, Trevor is dating the wrong girl. And you knew about it, but lied? Are you really okay with Trev dating Amy? Because I know for a fact that Amy doesn't even like Trevor. She's using him for me. She thinks she can brainwash me"

"Look, it doesn't matter if I'm okay with her or not. It depends on Trevor. And believe me, I've never seen him care for someone so dearly. I don't know about Amy but, Trevor really loves her. I just, don't want to spoil his happiness"

I groan "But why Amy? Out of eight billion people, why Amy?"

"Listen, she might have changed. You guys were really young that time. And she feels guilty for what she did. She might not be a good friend, but she might be better in a relationship"

I don't even wish to understand her, all I know that I have to protect my brother from that Darren. If I could, I would just walk to Trevor and tell him everything. But it isn't that easy. I just don't want to break his heart.

Blair is right, I've never seen Trevor so affectionate towards anyone. Maybe she changed herself for Trev. But I cannot let anything change my mind. There is a huge possibility that she wants to manipulate Trevor.

I have to do something that makes Amy leave, because I know that she doesn't have any affection for him. But I can't just walk up to him and spit it all out. I want Amy to tell him everything. I know it's gonna hurt him, but it's better than living in a lie.

I was lied to my whole life, and I know how bad it hurts.

Sage

"You guys met her?" Trevor asks turning away from his laptop. It's currently 9pm and we're still at the restaurant because it was a rush today.

I so wanna tell him about how I really feel about Amy but, I don't think it's a good idea. I thought about it a lot since the last time I saw her yesterday. Maybe I overreacted. I do have a point that I can't trust her, but I should have reacted more maturely. And I can understand because if we ignore what she did to me, she is really sweet and it's believable that anybody will fall for her.

But that's the trouble, we shall never ignore what she did to me. "Yeah, and I might say that she's incredible"

Blair looks at me. I can tell that she's relieved by my response. That's what I love about her. She always solves crisis calmly and maturely. Unlike me who always get hyper.

By the way Trevor has been so long, I can tell that Amy didn't tell him anything about how I treated her. Or maybe she is just trying to prove me how courteous she is. But no one knows her better than me.

"We shall leave now, it's late" Trevor closes his laptop. "By the way, shall we invite her for dinner tomorrow?"

I wanna say no, but I can't. Alright, I'll just tolerate her for a few days, until I think of something to get rid of her. "Definitely" I say. It might sound normal to Trev, but Blair can recognize my sarcasm.

We get out of our office and were about to leave the place. It's been really quiet here so our footsteps are pretty clearly heard. As I raise my head to continue walking, I stop. Clyder was just sitting on one of the tables casually. And it's obvious to me now, that Blair and Trevor can't see him.

He was piercing me with his eyes. He was looking at me as if we need to have a serious talk. I can tell by the look of his face that he knows. He knows that I know.

Something is dark in his look. Everything is dark in his look.

His eyes aren't filled with ocean anymore. Instead of reminding me how beautiful the ocean is, it reminds me how terrifying its depth is.

I don't even want to talk to him. While I was looking at him, Trev and Blair already got out. So it was just him and I. I try my best to pay no heed to him and walk away. But his words freeze me.

"You are giving Amy a chance to stab you again?"

I felt shivers down my body. It felt like I just encountered a serial killer. I turn my head towards him and exclaimed "What is that supposed to mean? And why do you have to talk about it anyway?"

I'm mad. Maybe because he lied. Or maybe because he is talking trash. Or maybe I'm just mad because of the things happening around just excluding him. I don't know. I'm mad because I'm heart-broken.

He stands up and walks towards me. "I said that I need to talk to you"

"That's not what you said" I felt as if my voice had no emotions. It sure didn't. I'm being arrogant, and that's exactly what I need to be.

"I'll say everything you want to hear, if only you're ready to lend me your ears, and surround me with questions"

I open the gate and shout "I'll be home in less than and hour"

"What are you going to do alone?" Blair yells backs. "Just had a little work and want a little alone time"

She says a word to Trevor and then they go. I close the gate and point towards the kitchen. I lead him there "You want questions? Well, I'm not searching for any answers. Is that valid?"

"No it's not. We have to sort this out"

I take out four slices of bread and start to toast them. There was silence in the kitchen. Then I turn towards him with my chin up. "Why?"

He looks at me confused. "What do you mean 'why'?"

I keep the toasts on a plate and then cook some ham. I say without looking at him "Why do we need to sort this out? Who are you? My family? My best friend? My boyfriend? Exactly, nothing."

I look up at him again after cooking the hams "You're my nothing. You're just a weird guy who has no name, and also has weird secrets. Plus, you're trying to get me attached to you, even though you know everything" I take out the condiments and start layering the sandwiches.

"Why do you think I know everything?"

"Maybe because you're the first person to ask nothing about my bracelet. Or maybe because you have a book of my life, that comes to be nothing but just an imagination…like you"

I take the two plates of sandwiches back to the table. We sit down and I slide a plate of sandwich to him. "You know I'm just an imagination?"

Why is he answering with questions that are actually repeating me? It's not attractive. I want him to be attractive. I don't respond to him because

I know he already knows the answer to that so I just take a bite of the sandwich. "Imagination" he says "It's such a beautiful place" then he takes a bite too.

I swallow and ask "I thought you prefer reality, as you once said"

He grins "That's because I have you in my reality, but you have me in your imagination" I roll my eyes "Imagination is just an excuse to escape the reality. It's not real"

"But it's still pretty. At least that's the place we're all happy in"

I stare him chewing his food while he was looking down at the plate. This is the first time after the wedding that we're having a serious conversation. Except that at the wedding we were happy. After a few seconds, I ask him "Who are you?"

He looks up at me and stares me before responding "Clyder"

"No" I answer almost immediately. "Clyder is just my imagination. Who are you?"

He inhales, and exhales. Then he looks down at the table while his tongue moving on his lower teeth. He looks at me and says "I already told you that I have no name. But I understand you're question." He gulps "You're actually asking who the person in you're dream was"

I nod because that's exactly what I'm asking. "That person was me, but the real me." I raise my eyebrows to show my interest, but I'm actually stunned. I shouldn't be because that's the obvious guess anybody would make. "So, the real *you* must have a name?" that sounded more like a question than a statement.

He nods but doesn't answer. I stare at him while he takes the last bite of his sandwich. He swallows and sits back straight.

"I can't tell you"

"I didn't ask"

"But I know you wanna know"

I groan and bang my hands lightly on the table "Clyder, please, speak to me clearly. I'm already stressed out and you're making me upset."

He closes his eyes and drops his head between his shoulders "You're not upset or stressed because of me or this new truth you just discovered"

I don't even want reactions and I don't want to react. I want simple answers. I just cover my eyes with my palms. We're talking like we're in a movie and we're repeating our scripts.

He looks at me deeply "You're stressed because of Amy and Trevor" I immediately open my eyes and look at him. I open my mouth to ask him how he has this information, but then stop because realization hit me. Of course he knows everything, because he is in this world to let me out of here. And he might know my past life in Ohio. I widen my eyes as I realize why he said that Ohio is nostalgic for him.

"You have no right to speak on this"

He looks down, and then back at me "I thought we were both each other's personal diaries" then he chuckles "That's correct, I have no right. But if you knew the bond we actually had, you would let me solve every single problem in your life"

I start to tear up. I stand up and say in a slightly louder voice "I do feel a bond with you, but not the way you feel with me. I know you're here to tell me to break the wristlet and go back to the other world to you" I was crying "It's not that easy Clyder, it isn't. I have my family here, I can't be selfish enough to leave them just so that I could live a peaceful and heavenly life there"

He nods very calmly. I can tell that he's trying to absorb everything. "That's right, I totally understand"

But I don't. I don't want him to understand. I want him to force me to run away to the other world. I wish I never asked mom about this wristlet. I wish I never knew that Clyder isn't real. I wish I just lived the way I wanted to, happy, with Blair and Trevor, away from Amy, with Clyder for life. But that isn't life. Life doesn't go according to you. Being happy isn't hard, but finding happiness is.

"I won't be selfish, Sage. But I also know that you're confused about this decision." I gulp. I'm thinking…*thinking wisely. Intensely. Deeply.* Minutes full of silence pass between, and I'm still thinking.

"Clyder," I finally say. He looks up at me "How do I break this wristlet?"

He stands up slowly and genuinely stares me "Are you sure?"

"No, I'm just eager to know. And if the universe wants me to return to that world, I surely will"

He gulps. I can see the confusion on his face. Then he sighs "You can't break the wristlet but, you can break its spell"

He walks away from me to the gate "You will have to take the real name of any person that exists on the other world" I turn my body towards him and fold my arms "Okay then, answer me, *who are you?*"

"Reagan," he says "*Reagan Knox*" and then he walks out.

Sage

I walk out of my room after taking a bath and getting ready for the dinner. Blair was laughing hard with her phone in her hand. Then she points at me "Oh," she chuckles "You're here" she is saying that like I came out of my room after days. She laughs again while beating the heck out of a pillow next to her on the couch.

"Are you drunk?" I ask her while I take a look on the food. "Sage, I don't drink" she says trying to control her laughter. This night is seriously scaring the hell out of me because I'm going to have a dinner night with Amy, and Blair there is laughing on a stupid meme. Well, *maybe* it's a meme.

She takes a huge breath and walk towards me. "The food's good right?" she asks "I don't know and I obviously don't care. I mean it's probably going to be delicious but, I'm not ready" she places her hand on my shoulder, "Yes you are, I believe you are and, you look great" she probably complimented because I was wearing the black puff sleeves shirt she gifted me once. "You should get ready too" She makes a funny face when she realized that she is still in a high messy bun in a messy outfit that has some stains on it. As soon as she leaves, Trevor comes out wearing a white shirt with its sleeves rolled up.

"Is everything ready?" he asks while setting his hair back. "Yeah, except Blair" he checks his phone to Amy's texts.

I have been quite distracted since yesterday so I haven't really thought about this dinner night. The conversation I had with Clyder last night kept my mind busy.

Reagan, actually.

I thought about it a lot. I came to the conclusion that the moments I've spent with Clyder, will be known by Reagan. That's obvious because, if I'm Valerie, Clyder is Reagan.

And if my guesses are right, I suppose that, just like Clyder, Valerie is also an imagination except for the fact that others can see her. That means there is no *Sage and Clyder* or *Valerie and Reagan* because Valerie and Clyder don't exist. So it's just *Sage and Reagan.*

That's a little complicated though. But these complicated thoughts are the reason I almost forgot about this night with Amy. And that's why I'm nervous now. But I shouldn't be because I did nothing wrong, except for how I reacted last time.

In a couple of minutes after we all are ready, she knocks on the door. Trevor face lit up and he rushes to open the door, Blair behind him. I kept sitting on a chair near the kitchen slab. Nervousness was rushing down my body. When I thought about how to react with her, I thought I will be confident, chin up and making extreme eye contact to make *her* nervous. But here I am, betraying myself and being a cowardly cat. I can see her arms hugging Trevor and Blair giving her a warm smile. Trevor leads her in the house holding her hand.

Literally holding hands.

Ridiculous.

As soon as she enters and sees me, her smile drops, as well as her gaze. I am trying my best to hold eye contact with her to show that I'm not ashamed of what I did earlier, even though I am. As expected, she's trying her best to pass up me.

The three of them are talking like they're best friends. *Like they're Amy, Blair and me.* "Sage, bother to come over?" he is still being sarcastic. Jeez.

"I got an important call, call me when ya'll take the weight off your feet for dinner" then I look towards Amy "It's marvelous to meet you again, Amy" and without a response, I hold my phone up to my ear, pretending to be on a call. I walk towards my room, but I don't shut it. I don't want Trevor to think I'm being rude.

I never thought I would have to talk to Amy again after that day. The day of the music contest. The day when she stabbed me. The day I told her that I hated her.

We were so young.

I sit on my bed and try to relax. I've never been so nervous and scared. Not even on my first day of school. Not even when I performed on a stage for the first time. Not even in a presentation. Not even in any interview. Not even with Clyder. The person, who once comforted me, is making me uneasy now.

"Distraction, distraction…" I mutter to myself as I close my eyes. And then luckily, my phone starts ringing.

Miracle.

It was Noah. "Hey what's up" I pick up.

"Well, something went wrong" of course, everything is going wrong. Today none of us visited the restaurant so we didn't know what's going on. "What's wrong?"

"Vandalism"

Oh god. That word is horrifying for restaurant owners. But I don't even own the restaurant. "You should tell Blair before me"

"She wasn't answering, and Trev's phone is switched off" well that's a coincidence. Good thing that they won't be disturbed with their Amy. "Is the vandalism major?"

"Not really. Actually, this morning, we only found broken windows"

"That's it? No spray painting or stolen appliances?"

"Nope. But this could get worse. We haven't checked the camera's yet"

"Good, we'll check it tomorrow, and lets see if they vandalize again this night" and then we hung up. Why is everything going wrong? I swear, Amy is a black cat.

I should now actually get out of my room or else Trevor will hate me. I won't be telling anyone about the vandalism because I don't wanna ruin Trevor's night. And I really hope I don't lose my temper on the table.

"Okay, I'm literally starving" said Blair walking towards the kitchen. "I know right. Let me help you set up the table" Amy walked behind her. Trevor looked at me and took a seat on the table "Come on"

A minute later, we all were on the table. "Wow, four seats full, feels just like a family. We need to get used to it" Trevor says pouring himself a glass of soft drink. I wanna apologize to break his heart but, we won't be getting used to it sweetie. This young lady, namely Amy Darren, who's sitting right in front of me, won't be a forever thing.

"Thank you so much for this dinner night. It's been so long since I've sat with a family" she says it looking at Trev and Blair. Well hello? I'm sitting right in front of her. She should be thankful to me for not punching her right now. And she knows very well how experienced I am with punching noses. "Yeah right" I mutter faintly, but it still draws everyone's attention to me. I wanna mortify her so bad right now.

"Amy," I say energized "Please tell us about your high school life. I wanna know so much more about my to-be sister-in-law"

Blair stares me as if I just cursed her. Amy looks down at her plate "Um, well"

"Yeah?" I say watching her intensely. She sighs "I d…don't know" okay but seriously, I wanna laugh so bad right now.

"Sage, actually, there was a tragedy that occurred with her earlier" Trevor interrupts. Tragedy? That occurred with me, not her.

"I got into a car accident, few years ago" she gulps "The accident was major. It was night time and my mom and I were returning home from somewhere, that's when the accident came about" then she looks up at me "My mom and I both survived but the doctor told me that, the accident caused me Amnesia"

What.

Oh God. This isn't happening. No this can't happen. My life is literally a disaster. I can't help myself staring at her. I look at Blair but, she isn't shocked as I am. She just looks at me, then down at her plate.

She knew it.

She knew about it, but didn't tell me. Why? Oh my goodness, I feel so bad. That means Amy doesn't remember anything about me. I talked so junk about her that day. She might think I'm a psycho. But if Blair already knew, why didn't she tell me?

No wonder Amy is a doctor instead of a lawyer.

Blair tries to change the subject and that made all of them engaged in another conversation. I couldn't help it but drop my head, ashamed of how I behaved.

This is so ridiculous. I feel so awful. Amy went through so much after I left her. I don't know how to feel about it. I have no clue how to react.

After a few minutes after the dinner, Amy and Trev were on the couch discussing something, and Blair and I were in the kitchen.

"You knew it" I say to her, trying to look in her eyes. She was avoiding every eye contact I was trying to make. "Blair, look at me"

"I'm sorry" she says looking down at her feet with her hands on the kitchen slab. I sigh "You did nothing wrong, there's no need to apologize, seriously"

Then she finally looks up at me waiting for me to say something. I cross my arms and chew on my lower lip. Then I inhale "Why didn't you tell me?"

"Because," she pauses "I don't know. I'm seriously so screwed. As I said, I want Trev and Amy to be together, but I knew how bad it would hurt you, so I let you yell at her"

That was a bad decision. She can't do that, seriously. "Sage, I know that, even though you know that she doesn't remember anything about what happened with you that time, you won't accept her"

"I can accept her but I don't want to. I know she has lost her memory but she still is Amy Darren. She lost her memory, not her mindset. She's still that Amy who stabbed me"

She looks down for a few seconds. "Can I say something?" she asks without looking at me. I raise an eyebrow as to why she's asking that.

"The night you called me and told me about what Amy did to you, I was in shock. And I would have punched her teeth if I was there. I hated Amy for almost forever after then. But as I grew up, I realized how young we were. It was a stupid mistake. She was just scared. Scared of her mother. Scared of getting expelled and letting her own mother ruin her future. Scared of getting the same life as her mother."

"What she did was worth calling cops. And besides, I want to forgive her but, it isn't easy"

"That's like being an imbecile. People light up their own people's houses and still are forgiven. She isn't a narcissistic."

"She locked me up in a dark room, letting me bleed all alone. What if Evelyn didn't show up?" I understand what Blair is trying to do. She isn't trying to support Amy, she actually just wants to show that, the past doesn't matter now.

She walks to the other side of the kitchen slab, right in front of me "Okay, imagine being in her shoes. Imagine having no father and living with an abusive mother. Imagine your mother hates your best friend. Imagine you are getting a life full of abuse and being unloved. Imagine you want a better life by working hard for your future. Imagine your mother threatens you that if you get expelled, she won't be paying for your education and will make it hard for you to grow into a better and richer human being. Imagine the school bully terrorize you that if your best friend doesn't get expelled, you will. Imagine the pressure. Imagine the fear. Imagine the confusion. *Imagine, Sage*"

I am speechless. I just stare at her with tears. There was a time when I felt more than this for Amy. I always wished I could carry her pain. But, I have words "Okay, Blair. Now imagine being in *my shoes*. Imagine having a best friend that's with you your whole childhood. Imagine you love her more than anything in your whole life. Imagine how closely you're attached with her. Imagine believing that you both are soul sisters. Imagine having a best friend that you used to call at midnight crying about your pain, and her comforting you like the whole world is now heaven. Imagine her trying to make everything better in your life. Imagine you got into a big trouble where the bully is threatening you that she'll get you expelled. Imagine the atmosphere where you know that if you get expelled, you will have to break every contact with your best friend. Imagine you realized your best friend, the one you were fighting for, the one you loved the most, the one you were risking your future for, *stabbed you* for her goodness. Imagine your best friend betraying you. *Imagine, Blair*"

I want to say so much more than just this like, *Imagine being told that you're not from this world and were kept away from your sister your whole life without being told the reason. Imagine being told that the guy you actually started liking is your soul mate but from another world and you accidently like your own imagination. Imagine realizing that you have to choose between your family and your soul mate that lives in your mother land.*

Blair nods. Still nodding, she says "I understand"

"Of course you do" I hold her hands "You do understand. You're the only one who understands me. We never even had a deep bond before, but still, it was just you who healed me"

She gives me a soft smile, then stands up straight and says casually

"Alright so, what are you gonna do about Amy? I mean, will you accept her, because you don't have a choice"

Good question. Or maybe, good thought. "I will accept her for Trevor, but I won't forgive her. I won't really make a friendly bond with her, but I won't hurt her"

"I get it. And by the way, whose call did you get earlier" I won't tell her that I faked it, because first I did fake it, but then I actually got a call. I should probably tell her now. "It was Noah. He informed me that our restaurant got vandalized"

"What?" she widens her eyes. "It's just broken windows. They haven't checked the cameras yet. We will tomorrow, hopefully"

She sighs and stretches her arms. "Blair" Amy calls her from behind. She and Trevor are now near the door. "I need to leave now. Thank you so much for the dinner, it was appetizing." Trevor was also going behind to drop her home.

"Wait," I call from behind "I want to drop Amy home" I don't know why I said that but I guess this way I can explain her why I behaved like that. Blair turns to me and gives me an *are-you-sure* look. I nod assuring her.

"That would be amazing. I swear ya'll three would become best friends over time"

Amy laughs at Trevor's statement, but I want to cry. Was that necessary for him to say? Blair places her hands on my shoulder and tilts her head, pointing me to go with her now.

We leave for the car.

My dream low-key came true. I mean, I used to wish that once I get my drivers license, Amy and I would go on a long drive together. Even though this dream shattered after that day, and even though the circumstances are way different now, *we are in a car together.* When I was thirteen years old, I pictured us being in a car, driving on an empty road at night, blasting Taylor's songs inside and singing on the top of our lungs, knowing that the next day she'll be working in a court and I'll be in my office in my own company.

However, this never happened. Yes we are together in a car. Yes its night time. Yes the road is empty. But no we're not playing songs. No we're not singing. And she's actually going to be working in a hospital tomorrow, and I'll be checking security cameras to see who vandalized our restaurant. Oh wait, it isn't even my restaurant.

Both of us, Amy and Sage, are once again together. But this time, she doesn't remember the memories we created over years, and I just don't want to remember any.

"I live in Daisy Apartment" she tells me. That's an expensive one though. "You're mom is still in Ohio?"

"No, she lives with me. I own a whole floor" damn, she's rich. "I will soon leave the apartment because I don't want to live with her. After we came from Ohio, we…" she pauses and looks at me "Wait, how do you know I came from Ohio? I didn't tell Trevor about it"

Okay so we're finally at this topic now. "Well, long story short, I knew you before you started dating Trevor." She keeps staring me so I go more in detail "You and I had some history before you lost your memory"

She raises her eyebrows "Oh, were we friends?"

I don't want to tell her what she did to me, because our memory is the main one in her brain. If she comes to remember it, it might cure her Amnesia. It's not that I don't want her to heal but, now she's living her best life as a doctor. And she might regret all her decisions after.

She's living her best life because she stabbed me.

And if someone can stab their *own best friend* and leave them in a dark room all alone so that they can make their own future, they can definitely kill other people for their own profit.

"No, we were just classmates. We got into a fight in high school. Since then I didn't liked you much"

She widens her eyes and says in a louder voice "Oh! That's why that day you…" "Yes" I interrupted her "That's why I yelled at you"

She nods as she's to express that now she gets it. "But you said that you're gonna stab me like *I did*. Did I stab you back then?"

Wow, I said that? I was really angry that time. How am I supposed to answer that? Amy is asking *'Did I stab you?'*. How can I possibly answer that?

"I don't remember saying something like that"

She stops with her questions and chews on her lower lip. Then she chuckles. My heart is melting after seeing her laugh. It's been so long since I heard it.

When she was gone all those years, I always wanted to hate her, know my worth and get over her. But it was like I always wanted to stay on those dark and gloomy thoughts about her. I never wanted to forget her, even though it hurts me. But now that she's back, I don't even know whether I should hate her or forgive her because of the accident.

The real question is, am I a monster or a victim myself?

"Were we close before the fight?"

"What?"

She clears her throat "Were we like, seatmates or group mates that were close or did we always hated each other?" She really doesn't have to be so interested in these thoughts. I don't want to lie more "We neither hated each other, nor we were close. We just had nothing to do with each other and that's the last question I'm answering" She looks outside the window. After a few seconds, she asks again "Alright so were we like…"

"Holy biscuits Amy. How many questions do you have?"

She starts laughing. No I'm not laughing and I don't want to. "What's *holy biscuits?*" what an absolutely fascinating question. "Just a habit. I learned it from that video, remember?"

She stops laughing. "Sage, I don't remember any video" oh yeah, I forgot. I actually learned it from a random video that was hilarious. And *holy biscuits* was our inside joke that turned into a habit over time. I forgot that she doesn't remember it.

"Forget it. It's just a habit"

I turn the car towards her apartment. As soon as she got out, I decided to leave as fast as possible. But then I saw Ms. Darren near another lady doing some chit chatting.

Oh no. If Ms. Darren comes to know that Amy is dating my cousin, she would never approve Trevor. And I know that Ms. Darren will never remind Amy about me.

"Amy!" I stop her. She comes back and leans on the car window. "Listen, you're mom hates me, so don't tell her about me or Blair."

"Why does she hate you?"

"What sort of mother would like a girl who fought with her daughter?" she laughs and nods, going back inside. Well, Ms. Darren would never care even if someone punched her.

Sage

I doubt myself. I said that I won't mess with Trevor and Amy but I won't forgive her. What if it's just an excuse? What if I'm saying it because I want Amy in present? What if I still love her?

I am supposed to return home after dropping Amy but I'm burnt out. I don't know if I'm over thinking or under thinking. My mind is scrambled. I need another alone time.

I was playing Reckless by Madison Beer. When ever I heard a breakup song or a song about a girl being cheated on, it reminds me about Amy. Strange huh? The song just has one of the most beautiful lyrics.

I guess my friends were right...

Each day goes by and each night, I cry,

Somebody saw you with her last night,

You gave me your word, "Don't worry 'bout her",

You might love her now, but you loved me first.

Said you'll never hurt me, but here we are...

I have a habit of changing the lyrics of certain songs so that I can relate to them.

I guess my sister was right...

Each day goes by and each night I cry,

Nobody saw you stab me that time,

You gave me your word "Forever we're one"

You might slip me now, but you loved me first,

Said you'll never hurt me, but here we are…

I forgot to do my homework, when I was six. It was the first week of the second term in first grade. We had to color a drawing of a house. I could have done the homework in five minutes just sitting there while the teacher checked other student's notebooks. But I forgot to bring my crayons, so I just sat there and cried. I was always a cry baby. I knew the teacher would write a complain in my diary, and even though I knew that mom and dad won't scold me, I wanted my diary's *teacher's remarks section* empty. That's when my new seat mate looked at me.

"Why are you crying?" she asked me.

"I forgot to do my homework"

"Okay then tell the teacher that your dog ate it"

I sob "But I don't even have a dog" she pulled my notebook towards her "I will help you color it fast"

I wipe my tears "Really?"

"Yes!"

I swear I'm so lucky that I didn't complete my homework that day, or else I was always too shy to talk to any other students.

"My name is Sage, and what's yours?"

"I'm Amy, and I like Pegasus"

"Wow, I love unicorns. Do you watch *my little pony*?"

"Yes, it's my favorite cartoon!"

Ands that's how, we had silly conversations that led us to be best friends, not so forever I guess.

After a few days, Amy invited me to her house, and I was never so excited before. That night when I saw her mom, I felt like I was in a horror movie.

"Where is your dad?" I whispered to her after a few minutes into her house. I expected her dad to be like Amy. Sweet, funny and pretty.

"Mom said that demons ate him up because he was a bad kid who never did his homework and never listened to his mom"

Till this day, I still can't believe how any mother could say such a disturbing thing to a six years old.

We were always so funny together. We were together for about ten years. That just means one thing, that I loved her more than she loved me. Her mom probably brain washed her. Those twenty minutes were the most miserable minutes of my life.

Our story ended in the most horrible and heartbreaking way possible, but it's still the best one I know.

All these years, the only lesson I learned is that, everyone is replaceable, every single one of them. Whether it's your sibling, teacher, cousin, relative, boyfriend, girlfriend and even your best friend, at the end of the story, it's just you and you. We were sent on earth alone, we're going back alone.

I won't say that everyone is the same, I'm just telling that I never experienced *"I will be with you till your last breathe"*

Sage

"Holy biscuits, she's pretty" as I said that, Trevor looks at me "You can't be serious right now"

We were going through the cameras and we found out who vandalized the restaurant. It was a little girl. She looked about nine years old. "We can't call the cops on a little girl"

She looks so delightful. In the camera, she was purposely showing her face. Her red hood covered her body and we could only see a little of her front hair that was orange, or maybe golden like honey. And she had freckles, just like Trevor. She was smiling and waving at the camera after breaking the windows. I found myself laughing at her.

"She didn't show up last night. Does that mean it was a one time thing?" Blair said looking at Trevor. Noah stands up and says "If this happens again, we'll call the cops just to find her parents. Let's forget it for now"

That's kind of weird, I mean, why would a child just vandalize our restaurant? We don't even know her. She's a child and she's literally smiling at the camera, as if she *wants* to get caught.

"Oh well" Trev walks away. From the past months, I learned that Trevor's *Oh well* doesn't mean *it is what it is*. It meant that *I'm pissed off and leave me alone.*

Maybe I'm not that concerned about that vandalism because it's not my own restaurant. But it is still somehow *like* my own.

The restaurant hasn't opened yet, so it's just four of us. So we just start early.

Being in a restaurant is fun and stressful at the same time. It's fun to see adorable families visit the restaurant for a dinner night. But it's greatly annoying to see high school kids just screaming and yelling while celebrating some sort of crap. Last weekend, a group of fourteen years old boys celebrated their friend's birthday. It was all fun until other customers started complaining about how disturbing they were. If it wasn't enough, they almost broke into a food fight. They treat restaurants as if it's their school cafeteria.

And on another Sunday, I was really burnt out. It was 8pm and I wanted to go home half an hour early. I was about to tell Blair, but then a trio of girls just entered. That's when Trevor told me to take care of them. If I had the energy, I would punch his face.

I wonder why I love punching so much.

I kept an eye on them while they ordered something. But all I could here was giggling and laughing. After ten minutes, their waitress comes up to me tells me that they are ordering wine but they forgot their ID at home. And they are being stubborn. So I went to check up on them. I asked them what can I get them and they ordered wine. When I asked for their ID to verify their age, they started laughing and said they forgot their ID at home. My blood was boiling at that time, but we somehow got rid of them.

The restaurant had opened an hour ago, when I see mom enter. She looked thrilled by looking at the restaurant. Blair went up to her and hugged her. Mom looked so overjoyed talking to Blair. Then she spots me while I saw giving company to the customers. She comes up to me and hugs me too "It's so spectacular" she says roaming her eyes around. She has seen the pictures of the restaurant but it's her first time visiting it. She looks back at me "Are you okay?"

At first I get confused by why she's asking that but then I commit to memory our last conversation. When the truth got unwrapped.

I look down to avoid her eye contact. I sigh and nod, but I lied. I'm not okay. "Why don't you have a seat, I'll be back in about ten minutes. Do you want something to eat? A drink perhaps?"

"No I'm good"

I spend the next ten minutes pointing out the waiters and helping them, and welcoming customers. I came back to her seat with a cup of latte for her.

"You looked so elegant there" she said and that made me smile. She takes a sip and says "I have something to show you and this latte is delicious"

"Thanks and what do you wanna show?"

She opens her purse and takes out an old purple notebook. As soon as I saw stickers of flowers stick on it, I recognize it. It's one of my old journals. I immediately take it "Where in the holy biscuits did you find it?" my eyes were widening to look at it because I thought I lost it years ago. It has so many memories written on it. It's heart melting.

"It was inside a pillow case back in Ohio"

Oh yeah, once I knew Lyn was coming over, I hided it inside a pillow case so she won't find it. *I guess no one ever found it until mom did.* "Don't worry, I didn't read it" Good because it would be so mortifying.

I open a random page from the middle to read it

Dear Diary,

Today we got McDonalds. And for the first time, I tried the Quarter pounder burger with cheese and bacon. I've never ate such an appetizing burger ever. But because of that, dad said I can't have Mcnuggets because that would be too much. Next time I'm coming here, I'm getting the Twix Mcflurry and that's it.

I chuckle "I still didn't get the Mcflurry I wanted back then" I turn to another page and read it while mom was still enjoying her latte.

Dear Diary,

Today we had a food fight at school. And guess who started it, Amy and I. Yeah, quite chucklesome. So it started when Brad accidently threw his sandwich on Ralph. Amy thought they were having a food fight, so she threw her whole lunch on him. So I yelled "FOOD FIGHT!!" and everyone went bananas. Speaking of bananas, Amy and I were covered up in bananas by the end of the fight. But it was Brad and Ralph who got detention instead of us. My favorite part was when I saw Carrie pouring a whole bottle of orange juice on Chloe by accident. Her face was amusing that instant. If that wasn't enough, Amy also threw an avocado toast on Mr. Ray but we were so good at blending in, no one even noticed us. Might be the most hilarious day of seventh grade.

And then there was a picture of Amy and I covered up in bananas and milk. I wish it didn't, but it made me laugh. "Is that me?" a voice comes from right behind me. I closed the journal very instant "What are you doing here Amy? Aren't you supposed to be at the hospital? And no, that's not you"

She takes a seat beside mom. "My shift starts in an hour. Can I also get a latte, I'm really exhausted". I turn around and point at the waitress to get another cup of latte. "Hi, I'm Amy. I can tell you're Sage's mom. You both look so indistinguishable"

Amy always used to say that earlier, how my mom and I are one and the same. Mom stares her as if she's a psycho. Then turns to me and raises her eyebrows. I take a long breathe and say "She already knows you, Amy. Mom, this is Trevor's girlfriend" I say with a weird and sarcastically fake smile. My mom half nods and smiles at her, looking back at me with her eyes widen. "Mom, you needed to go meet someone, right?" I say, trying my best not to look suspicious. I don't want Mom and Amy to interact like this. My mom is well disciplined, unlike Ms. Darren, so she is still calm right now. But I still don't want them to talk, at least not like this.

Mom understands what I'm trying to do "Oh, um, yeah absolutely. Thanks for the latte"

I stand up "I'll walk to her car, and be right back" Amy kept eyeing us as we walk out the gate.

"What the hell was that?" mom asks me. I open her car gate and make her sit and I sit beside her. I explain her everything about what happened to Amy.

"Poor thing. I want to say it's karma but still, that's so unfortunate of her"

"You don't have to be so nice mom. Whatever it is, it is what it is. I told her we've met in high school, but I refuse to tell her more about each other, other than being classmates."

She nods "Makes sense"

I don't even know what I'm doing. I'm feeling like I'm lying to myself. From the day she said she wants me to hate her, I was totally shattered. Shattered in millions of pieces, and each and every piece is arguing with each other. A part of me says to forgive her, and a part of me says to totally cut her off. Whatever I do, I will betray myself. I'm stuck. I don't want to forgive her at all, but I don't want to cut her off.

It's not that I love her presence. Her presence still has the same darkness, same maliciousness and same brutality. Even when she's smiling at me, not knowing anything at all. I don't want to cut her off because off Trevor. It totally makes sense why he is dating her, but the fact that I can't tell Trevor anything, and I can't avoid Amy is killing.

I go back inside and roam my eyes around, unable to find Amy. She might be in our office.

I go back inside to find Blair and Amy giggling about something. Apparently, only Amy is giggling. Blair is just forcing a smile. When Amy turns towards me, she says ecstatically "Sage! I have a perfect plan for my engagement"

Engagement? Why are they rushing things? "Woah, slow down. You've already decided the engagement?"

"Yeah, few minutes ago" she still has the same enthusiasm like before. I don't like it. "I want you to play a song on our engagement party. I'll love to see you play guitar" I stare her in disbelief. It feels like she's a kid who's asking me to do stupid and dumb things. "I don't play guitar" I lie, wounding her with my look. I'm not exactly lying because I haven't played guitar since that day few years ago. "Oh come on, Trevor told me you know how to play guitar"

"I *knew* how to play a guitar" I correct her "I don't play guitar, *anymore*" I sit down on the couch beside Blair and open my laptop to complete my pending work. "Sage, please. I love guitar. I would really appreciate you"

I sigh "No, Amy". She sits beside me "Please…"

I stand up and thunder in a louder and sharper voice "No doesn't mean *convince me.* No means *No*"

"Relax. You don't have to yell" Trevor comes from behind me. "If you don't wanna play, just don't. Stop being so rude"

I just stand there when he returns back to work after saying something he shouldn't have. I am being rude because she's taking advantage of my kindness. Amy stands up and says in a lower voice "Can I at least get your number?"

I wanted to say *I'd rather jump off a cliff* but instead I say "No and I hope you don't try to convince me again" and I just walk away from there.

Sage

Dear Diary,

Today might be the most interesting day of my life, except my last birthday because that was legit insanely crazy. Today was interesting but, not in a good way. I don't even want to express anything, so I hope I burn this page, and all memories related to this day.

This was written few years ago, and I still remember the day. I can still never forgive myself for what I was about to do to Emma. I still wonder where Chloe might be. I always think about it, about school bullies. Do they realize their mistake? Do they believe they were wrong? Do they wish to apologize to the victims? Or do they just laugh about it?

I was sitting on my couch, Trevor was at the restaurant and Blair was managing online sitting on the dining table with her laptop. I open a new page and start writing.

Dear Clyder,

I wish I could call you Reagan, but I barely know him. I only know Clyder. Yes I know that both are the same. Or maybe, there's only Reagan and no Clyder. But it's hard to forget him, so I'll just call you Clyder.

This is the first letter I'm writing to you, and I'm not sure if it will reach you or not. I just needed someone I could talk to. I don't want a reply to this letter, I'm writing it to clear my mind.

I wonder how our reaction would be when we meet, only if we actually meet. I've known how to make it to the other world, but I'm still unsure if I really should.

It's been tough here lately, and the only thing that gave me ease was your presence. I always wondered why. This question was always stuck with me, why do I feel attached to you? But I think I got the answer to that.

Well, since you already know what's up with my life and you also know Amy, I want to talk to you about it. I know you can't do anything, but still.

Amy is back, as you know. But I'm confused and stuck. I don't want her here; I don't want to stay in contact with her. But Trevor and her are now getting engaged. I know that she doesn't remember a thing about us now, but I do. It's hurting me to have her in front of my eyes after years of hating her. I'm just her boyfriend's sister who she met few days ago so it shouldn't be hard for her to stay away from me. But she's my ex best friend whom I used to sneak out with, whom I had a sleepover with, whom I used to have a food fight with, whom I used to tell all my secrets to, whom I loved so very much, who I lost a few years ago.

The pain feels more than a breakup. It feels equivalent to being cheated on. Actually, I want to forgive her and become the same thing we were before. But I'm scared. The fear is still the same and it isn't that easy. It feels like I'm betraying myself by forgiving Amy.

Being sensitive sucks. I start crying on the most littlest things ever. I wish I was stronger. Stronger enough to handle this pain.

Damn, I shouldn't have let all of this out on you. It hurts because now that I know about that world, you can't stay here. I would still look forward to that day when you come to our restaurant, asking a table for one.

This might have made you bored right? Yeah I'll stop. The conclusion is that, reality is really depressing. And I really mean it.

Yours,

Sage

I tear the page out of the journal and fold it. I walk towards my room to find the red book and keep it inside it. If Clyder can send me letters through it, I can too. As soon as I keep the letter inside, I hear the door open. When I peek out my room, I see Amy. I swear she has been really quirky and annoying after Amnesia.

She looked tired so she immediately took a seat on the couch. I won't complain about her making herself comfortable here because it's actually good. "Coffee? I made three cups" Blair asks her. She nods "Yes, please"

I walk out the room to make a friendly atmosphere after what I did yesterday. I don't feel guilty at all, it's just for Trevor. "Being a doctor truly is hard" I say taking a seat beside her. She sits up straight "Yes exactly. Today I had a very annoying patient. She was complaining about every move I took and she called me a pillock"

I laugh "Just like Chloe"

"Yeah, exactly"

And boom. This was the moment I was waiting for so long. I want to laugh, but I'm hella angry. It feels like I planned this but it's nothing like that.

I ask her "What do you mean by exactly?"

"Exactly means, she really was like Chloe" that's when she realized, that she messed up badly. She stares at me frozen. I can see her gulp. I tilt my head to the side and ask "*How do you know Chloe?*"

That's when I felt Blair looking at us in disbelief, when she finally says "Amy?"

Amy removed her gaze and looked down at her feet, avoiding eye contact. "How mortifying, isn't it?" I ask her. The way she was sitting uncomfortably on the couch made me feel uncomfortable too. Yet she doesn't say a word.

She immediately stands up to leave. That's when I rush and close the door on her face before she left. She had fear in her eyes, the same fear she had when her mom used to hit her bad. But this time, I will not fall for it.

I start walking and backing her off "Do you have any explanation on this?" tears started flowing down her cheek when she realized she was helpless. I finally say "You faked this goddamn amnesia to freaking trick us?"

"YES I DID" she yells at me "What do you expect me to do? Do you think you would accept me if I just showed up at your house as Trevor's girlfriend? I didn't know he was your brother, but I *actually* love him and I'm not faking it. When we started dating and he told me that his sister is Blair, I was hurt so bad. But that didn't give me a reason to break up with him. But after you started accepting me when you came to know I had Amnesia, I was melted. I was as hurt as you were, and it felt nice having you near me. I deserve your anger, and I don't mind. But please, don't kick me out of here, I will never return to this house, just don't keep me away from Trevor" she was sobbing "I had no option"

The atmosphere was same as it was few years. I could hear the same words she said that day.

I am not doing this intentionally. I am forced to do this. Just remember that, no one has ever mattered to me, but you do, just remember that. And trust me, I never wanted to do this.

I felt the same rage and fury I felt back then "You are a moron, Amy. A cheat, a liar, a fraud!"

She inhaled, trying to control her tears "The villain will always be the villain, if the hero tells that story. And perhaps, villains are not born, they are made"

"You have so much info about villains, but villains don't target their own best friends. And I'd rather jump in a volcano than letting you be with Trevor" Blair walks up to us "Listen, we can sort this out, alright?"

"All of this was a play?" I ask squinting my eyes. "Maybe we really could sort this out, if only you were honest. I seriously can't believe you. That time when I first saw you there, weren't you a bit ashamed just showing up there? For god sake Amy, behave like a human!"

Amy looked humiliated and irritated at the same time. She screams at me again "Why can't you love me back? Don't you see that I'm trying?"

"Shut up Amy" Blair yells at her. I run my fingers through my hair "That time you were asking me to play guitar at your engagement party, how could you not feel any embarrassment at all?"

I sigh loudly and look down. For a few seconds, there was silence in the room. Then I point at Amy and say "You know, years ago I used to think that I haven't met anyone better than you. But now I swear, I can never meet anyone worse than you." Then I raise my voice and yell "Get out of here because I'm literally done looking at your face. You're the dumbest, wicked and viscous human being I've ever met"

"What is wrong with you?" someone shouts from behind. We look behind to find Trevor standing at the door. Holy biscuits, I don't know for how long he's been hearing us. He looks furious and his eyes are so dark, I could barely see the white part. His hands were literally in tight fists. He walks up to us and stands between me and Amy, facing me. It's like he's protecting Amy from me.

"Trev I was just…"

"Not a word, Sage, not a word" he yells at me that makes me flinch. I widen my eyes to see this angry and dark side of him. This is the first time he is yelling at me. "What the hell did you just call her? *Dumb? Wicked and viscous?* Are you freaking serious?" he yells louder this time that again makes me flinch. I'm too shocked and scared to say anything right now. I feel my eyes turning hot. I'm tearing up. "You've been extremely rude to her from the day you've met her. Any valid reason?" his eyes are extremely dark and sharp. His looks are bloodcurdling. I took all my courage and energy to scream "You're being a jerk!"

"I'm being a jerk?" he yells back "You're the one being monstrous here"

"Trevor!" Blair interrupts "Shut your goddamn mouth" Trevor just silently looks at me, who was looking down at my feet and crying. I was literally crying. Amy runs outside, getting Trevor behind her. While I stood there with no words to describe how it feels.

What, just, happened?

I feel like I'm starting to get a panic attack. My heart was pounding extremely hard and my palms were sweating. My vision was getting blurry because of so many tears. Suddenly I felt shortness of breathe. Blair noticed it immediately and made me sit down. She gave me a glass of water "Sage, calm down. I understand it's just a panic attack. It'll be over in a few minutes. It's normal, relax"

I don't have any panic disorder, so it's really random and unpredictable. I kept telling myself

Calm down

Calm down

Just a few more minutes

Relax

Take it easy

I close my eyes and stay in the same position for ten minutes while Blair rubs my back. My panic attack started fading away, but the pain is still the same. I was still crying. I'm calm now but......*My brother yelled so bad at me because of a girl who once stabbed me.* This is just so, *heart breaking.* I feel completely shattered. I'm not sure what is going to happen next. What I know is that I can't stay here a single minute. At least for now.

I took a deep breathe and exhaled "I'll be back"

"Where are you going?"

I don't know where I'm going, but I just want to be alone. "I'll be home soon"

"Sage, its night time and it's raining outside. It's not safe to be driving right now" I understand her but I just don't care. I grab the car key and leave. I saw Amy and Trevor talking in the garage, but I'm not going to be even looking at them. As soon as I got in the car, I heard Trevor call my name, but I just drove away.

This isn't fair at all. I don't know what hurts more. Amy lying once again or Trevor being furious on me for Amy. What hurts the most is that,

Amy might be right. She might not be lying when she said she isn't being fake with Trevor. And the fact that she was right about me not accepting her is painful. She was brutally honest. I love honesty, but not after you've been lying so bad.

The rain was light when I left the house, but now it's raining heavily. The road is empty, obviously because no one is out in such rain. It's dark. It's creepy. I've never taken so much pain at the same time. The day can't get any worse.

It suddenly became so dark that it was hard seeing anything, and the rain was so loud. Plus my face was all wet with tears. That's when I suddenly saw a little girl coming in front of the car. And the next thing I know, I lost my balance and the car crashed into something. The last thing I heard was glass breaking.

***

I'm unable to open my eyes. Am I dead? I still hear the rain, but I'm pretty sure it's been very long since the accident. I'm still panicking. My ears are ringing. I open my eyes slowly, and all I could see is a kid's dead body and blood. *So much blood.*

I close my eyes tightly and open it again to have a better look. The car's front glass has crashed and the kid's body was lying right in front of me. My head is feeling really dizzy. I touch my head and realize I'm all covered in blood. I want to scream and cry, but my face hurts so much, I can't even move it. Somehow, the rain was moving towards me and I was wet, and cold….freezing cold. My eyes were blurry, because blood was spilling all over my face. I could barely move.

"H…h…hey….w…wake u…u…up" I try my best to say it to the kid, but I was trembling and there is no way she would hear me in this loud and heavy rain. It was so dark and… I don't know what to do or where to go.

After using all of my strength, I move my hand to move the kid. When I remove her hair, I recognize her. It was the same girl who vandalized our restaurant. "K…k…kiddo…h…hey" Did I kill her? She's actually dead. I shake my head "no…no…no…" I'm really petrified… really, *really petrified.* I'm not sure what to do. I can't remember anything, I can't find my phone either. All I feel is pain. I shut my eyes again "I can't do this anymore" tears and blood flowing down my cheeks "I want to live, peacefully." I inhaled a large amount of air. *I killed a kid.*

I don't want to live anymore, but I don't want to die either. I just want a break from whatever is happening. I stop moving and speaking, and I lose hope……

Sage

I hear people talking, but I'm unable to hear it clearly. I feel like I'm surrounded by white light. *Am I in heaven?* I don't think so, because I still feel pain. I try to open my eyes, but I can't open my left eye. When I open my right eye, I realize that my left eye is covered with bandage.

I'm in a hospital. I see Trevor talking to the doctor. Last time I was here when I fainted, I felt nothing when I woke up. But I can't move my body now. My brain is blank. They haven't noticed that I woke up. I have an oxygen mask on, and my head is covered with bandage.

I close my eyes and try to think, something, anything, everything…

Amy…

Trevor…

Panic attack…

Rain…

Car accident…

Blood…

The little girl…

I suddenly cough, that brought their attention to me. "Oh you're awake" the doctor says that very casually, and removes my mask. I suppose my condition is better now. Trevor leaves a big and loud sigh of relief. I move my eyes around to spot a window. The sunlight is so bright. It's morning now? Blair enters the room and when she sees me awake, she runs over to me "Oh my god Sage, I told you not to go out" she was teared up. Then Trevor says "We went out to look for you last night…"

I've been hear the whole night? My mind is all scrambled up and I can't think of anything. I stare at a white chair that is kept on the other side of the room. I focus on it till I start to come in sense.

"No," I say "The little girl…" Blair looks at me confused, she was about to say, or ask something, when I shout "I KILLED HER"

"Sage, calm down, what are you talking about?" I start to sit down straight. Blair holds my shoulder "Sage slow down!"

"Blair, I killed her… I killed a kid"

"Sage, you didn't kill anyone, what are trying to say!?" Trevor said. I was breathing heavily. The doctor makes me lie down and says "You're panicking, please calm down"

"I killed her…" I keep repeating the same thing. "Sage! There was no one else except you near the accident" that's when I stop moving. "What do you mean?"

"I think you're just imagining stuff, there was no little girl near the car" No way that I'm imagining stuff, I mean I do imagine *a lot*, but this isn't the case. Now that I know about Reagan and my existence and stuff, I'm pretty sure I won't imagine stuff anymore for my awareness.

If they didn't found the body… where did she go? No, I'm pretty sure she's dead. I killed her. I can't do this anymore… I don't want to take this pain. And about Amy, no, no, *no*.

Everything is so messed up. I'm messed up. This is the craziest thing to ever happen to me. And I have stopped acting surprised to these things.

I still feel the urge to die, but I still wanna live. Conclusion, I need a break. I want to run away, for a week, or month. I want to start over, from scratch. I want to forget everything and everyone.

It would be so good if I knew which choices can lead to the best outcomes. But as I said, life doesn't go according to you.

Sage

"Sage, *Sage…*" I hear a voice calling me. I open my eyes, and what I see, makes my jaw drop. Everything is, white. Or maybe it's blank. "Where am I?" I say, when I realize that I'm standing and I'm not covered in bandages anymore. I feel alright. "You're dreaming, Sage" I hear someone say that, in my own voice. It's like, I'm talking to myself. And did she just say I'm dreaming?

"It's time for you to decide"

"Decide what?"

"Decide where you live" I guess they mean between the two worlds. "Just keep in mind that, you have your family here. Your parents, Blair and Trevor, and also Amy…"

The voice stops for a few seconds to let me decide. But, why *am* I deciding? I am supposed to choose my own life where I have my family and everything; I can't choose a random and strange world. I can't trust it. "Ay yo, why do I have to decide all of a sudden?"

"That's not an answer to my question"

"Yes, because I'm asking *you* a question" the voice sighs at my response "Here, or the other world. Time is ticking Sage"

"What do you mean by *time is ticking,* what happens when the time runs out?" It feels like I'm in a movie and everything is scripted. The voice sighs "Listen, please answer me"

Good enough. I want to choose to be Sage, but I'm curious about Valerie. And my life as Sage is already so messed up. "Remember when you said you wanted to runaway?"

They know it... I can start over, I have a chance. "But be careful Sage. By choosing the other world, you might be selfish. You're going to hurt the feeling of the people you've known, specially your parents"

"The other world" I say "What?"

"I said I choose the other world"

"You really trust it so much?"

"I just don't care..."

"Last chance Sage, you're about to change your life"

Then I try to pull out the bracelet, expecting it to slide out. But then I remember what Clyder told me, so I scream "REAGAN KNOX"

And the next thing I know, there is a bright light coming, as if I'm in a tunnel.

What is happening? What did I just do? How did I end up like this? The last normal thing that happened to me was the argument with Trevor and Amy... and then the accident and now I'm here.

I'm sorry mom, I'm sorry dad. I'm so sorry Blair, I'm sorry Trevor. I don't know why I'm doing this. I don't want to do it, but I had to. I have no clue what's going to happen next.

Sage

"STOP IT!" I think I regret making this decision. Everything is black. I can't see anything. Oh wait, *I should open my eyes. Silly me.*

Before opening my eyes, I wonder to myself. My gut feeling says I might be standing in the middle of a world war. Or maybe I might be standing in a prison. This world might be full of fantasy, with dragons and fairies, and maybe even unicorns. I'm trying to best to predict how it'll be. I'm still scared to face what I'm going to see.

Then I open my eyes and… I'm holding an ice cream cone in my hand. *A goddamn chocolate cone with sprinkles on it.* I mean it looks delicious though but, that was not at all what I was expecting. I look around and, *holy biscuits*…my jaw literally dropped. Am I in a Harry Potter book? The place is like a more clean and peaceful version of the Harry potter's place. But I don't see any magic around.

"Is it good?" the voice makes me flinch. When I see who it was, I felt like the most relaxed and happy person ever. It was Clyder, no, I mean Reagan. He looks different. His hair is sort of orange, like honey dip. He is wearing a black shirt with casual jeans. I've never seen him so well dressed. But he has the same blue eyes, filled with ocean.

"What's good?" I ask. He looked annoyed "The ice cream" I look back at the ice cream "Oh, um, yeah it is" then I take a bite. Holy biscuits and the baker, I've never eaten such a creamy and delicious ice cream, like *ever*. Then I look down at myself. I'm wearing a white skirt and a red cardigan. I've never wore a skirt before. I feel cute. "Now you go your home, I go mine. Bye bye" then he immediately turns around to leave. "Wait Clyder, I mean Reagan, stop"

He turns around and looks at me with a shocking expression "What did you just call me?" "Reagan?"

"You called me *Clyder?*" I don't know what to expect next, his expressions are unpredictable. I just keep quite till he stares me. "Wait, Sage?" I smile when he says that. His eyes grow wider and the next thing I know, he's holding my shoulder with an overexcited expression "Are you serious right now? God, I can't believe you actually did it!" and then he turns around and starts laughing in excitement.

I've never seen someone be so excited to see me. It melts my heart. I don't know what to do next. Then he stops and says "What changed your mind?"

That's a tough question, or maybe the answer is tough. When I don't answer him, he nods "Never mind, forget it. What matters now is that you're here. You don't realize how excited I am to introduce everyone to you" I'm not sure if I'm supposed to be excited or nervous. I hope nothing goes too fast. "Wait, let's discuss it in my car. I'll tell you everything about this place in detail" he says and starts walking. He points at a car. "Wow, that's your car? It looks so expensive"

"No it isn't, it's an electric car actually- pollution free. Everyone has it. We don't have different cars like Toyota, Mercedes, Porsche and more. We have only one kind of car, electric cars. That's what makes this earth more peaceful than the other one because it's really, really low on pollution."

I'm already in love with this place. "Can we instead go on a walk, I wanna see more of this place" he nods.

I notice that this place is a mixture of city and village. It's like, roads with electric cars, in a beautiful village. And he's right, there's no pollution. The roads are made up of stones. There are lots of things made up of stone. The trees aren't like the one in our earth, they're prettier and greener. I wish I had spent my whole life here. "So this is where you live" I say looking around "It's so awkward, I don't know what I'm supposed to do like, I came here five minutes ago" he nods and says "Well, what *are* we supposed to do then? Trust me, you'll get used to living here in less than a day" he sighs like he just walked out of a storm leaving every stress behind, which I suppose is a *I'm so relieved and glad* sigh. "One thing you can do to make yourself more familiar is asking me questions about me and this place" then he laughs again out of excitement. It's adorable.

I laugh with him "Okay, alright, so how do you earn?" there comes my first question.

"Selling fruits" he says.

"Selling fruits? Are you serious?" he laughs. "Actually, things are really cheap here. For example, a cup of Starbucks hot chocolate costs 2.75 dollars in your earth. But it only costs less than a dollar here. You get the idea what I mean"

Wow, seriously, everything here is incredible. "So which magic school did you go to?" I ask him. He turns to me with a confused expression "What?"

I stare at him for a while, trying to think if I said something wrong.

When he realizes what I meant he again laughs hard. Am I really that funny? "Sage, this isn't a fantasy world. It's just as normal as your earth, it's just…better"

Maybe I should lower my expectations. We kept walking for several minutes while he gives me an introduction of the people around. And I realized how famous and well known he is. Not that he's a celebrity, but wherever he goes, he's just greeted and appreciated a lot. He knows everyone around here. "Reagan, where's Valerie?" I ask him out of curiosity. He sighs and asks me instead "Sage, where's Clyder?"

"Isn't it you? You're Clyder"

"Exactly. Just like that, you're Valerie" he looks up and says "I guess you're confused" I nod because I am. "Look, it's really simple. Actually, here, we don't fall in love. Before our birth, the future tells us who we are going to end up with. It was me with Valerie. But for some reason, I never felt any affection towards her, until I came to know about you"

Now it makes sense, it's so beautiful to know it. It's like, soul mates. He stretches his arms and yawns "You know, I still stayed with Valerie because I had this little expectation of you returning. And when the Elshers came to know about you, they sent me to your earth. But they forbid me from telling my name to anyone. That's how I ended up as Clyder" he smiles.

"Who are Elshers?" he stops walking and points up at something, not directly up at sky. I look towards where he's pointing and, I'm delighted. It's a *castle*. It's a massive and stunning castle. I'm literally thunderstruck.

"They are the rulers of the country. Royalty." I realized that the place isn't like Harry potter. It's more like Dunwiddie, from Sofia the first. "We have King Jasper Elsher and Queen Thora Elsher. And their *not so* nice son, Prince Truett Elsher, which happens to be my age"

After exploring for half-n-hour this place, nothing feels extraordinary. "Why is Truett *not so* nice?" I ask.

"He's just rude and spoiled, you know. He's always ready to punish people. I don't know what's gonna happen when he'll be the next King."

My legs are hurting after exploring so much. He's been talking so much about this place and he is extremely excited to spend everyday having me here. I feel like my legs have turned into stone "Can we sit down now?" he nods and enters a coffee shop.

Holy biscuits, it's so pretty. My eyes are blessed. "Coffee?" he asks. "Nope, I'm good" it surprises me because I haven't eaten anything for hours after the accident. Just an ice cream cone. Talking about the accident, it feels so good now. I can now say that I absolutely nothing to worry about. I'm about to live another life that is going to be completely different from my previous one. This is so exciting!

"Reagan" someone says from behind. He turns around and says "Oh, you're here too, come on" It was a kid, who looked about fifteen or sixteen. "Sage, this is Ellery, my sister" she was wearing a black hood that covered her body, not her brown hair. She had faint freckles on her face. She was just as beautiful as Reagan. "Sage? She's Valerie what are you talking about?" she says. Her eyes are pure black and dark, unlike Reagan's.

"Ell, I told you about it"

"Oh so she finally did it. Hi. It's magnificent to finally have you here" she isn't even smiling. It's giving me creepy vibes. "It's wonderful to meet you too"

"Frankly my dear, I don't give a damn" she says it so confidently as if it's normal for her to be so rude. "Ellery," Reagan glares her. "Do I get bonus points if I act like I'm scared?" wow, she's a baddie.

"Ignore her, she's always grumpy"

"He's always an ignoramus" she replies. I should take classes from her. "Whatever," he says. "What are you doing?"

"Am I not allowed to enter coffee shops?" she raises and eyebrow and pushes her hair back "Homework, jerk"

"Stop calling me that" then he turns to me "So, how did you end up here?"

"Well, I broke the spell, as you told me to. I felt like I should do it because, my life there got super messed up"

Ellery chuckles. She's way prettier when she smiles "So you ran away from your responsibilities? What a poltroon, more like a recreant" even though she just insulted me, I love the way she talks. Her accent is interesting. "What's a poltroon and recreant?" I ask.

"A coward! You're asinine" her vocabulary is insanely good. I know I must take classes from her. Reagan continued to tell me more about here. Like about how he sells fruits, about his friends, his family and his lifestyle. That's when I placed my hand on my skirt's pocket and realized I had something in it. I took it out a little bit to see what it is.

It was my bracelet. I'm not wearing it anymore. It feels and looks so weird having it outside my wrist. I never thought I would be able to see this view. This feeling is just indescribable. And the fact that I'm starting over is incredible.

I have nothing to worry about, I'm going to start a new life, in a heavenly place. I won't get those terrible and horrifying nightmares. Happiness felt like the first rays of timid sunlight after a winter storm, and by chasing the warmth of the sunlight, I could finally escape the internal dark and cold.

"Reagan!" I take out the bracelet "This pain in the asshole is no longer on me" I thought he's gonna be as excited as I am, but I was wrong. He immediately snatched it from my hand and it made me flinch. Ellery had the same expression of shock and fear. "What happened?" I asked. I swear I might be looking like an idiot.

He hides the bracelet under the table by covering it with his hands. He looks around and gulps. "Sage," he whispers "Where did you get this from?"

I hesitate "It was in my pocket"

He takes a deep breathe and clears his throat "This is forbidden" I widen my eyes "What's forbidden here?"

"The bracelet, you mob-headed twerp" Ellery states. Reagan puts it inside his pocket and tilts his head, motioning us to leave. "We'll discuss it in my car"

The whole time we walked to his car, I was terrified. I hope it's nothing very serious. Why is the bracelet forbidden? I felt like hundreds of dogs were barking at me and they can eat me out anytime. We were very silent, and awkward.

I wasn't accurately wrong when I assumed this place will be like a fantasy. When we're finally at in his car, me and Reagan in front and Ellery in the backseat, she shouts "You're so negligent. Are you a complete imbecile?"

I've suddenly forgot to respond to certain things. "Alright," Reagan finally says "Look, this bracelet isn't from this world, that's why it's forbidden. You only broke the spell, that's why you still have"

"But, you're the one who told me to…" "I know!" he interrupts "I didn't know this would happen"

I look away from him. I just came here an hour ago and I already committed a crime. I don't even know what will happen now. There's silence in the car. I think I brought stress instead of happiness to them.

"So," I ask "What will happen now?" Ellery speaks "Well, you're gonna get annihilated" I stare at her when I ask "What's annihilated?"

"To be destroyed, or killed"

"WHAT?" I came here to live a new life, and I'm about to get killed? What in the holy biscuits is wrong with my fate? I hold Reagan arms and panic "Reagan! What am I gonna do? They're gonna kill me!"

"Hey, hey, hey! Relax, she's just kidding" I turn my head towards her. She isn't laughing or smiling. "I don't jest around with people. I'm not kidding; I'm just trying to intimidate you for divertissement"

I'm angry but I'm too shaken up to yell at her. It was like I almost got thrown in a hippopotamus's mouth. "You might be sentenced to prison, for a very long time" he says "but only if the Elshers come to know about it"

I look at him, trying to get what he's trying to say "So, you mean, we'll have to hide it? Like people hide drugs?"

"And dead bodies" Ellery adds. "We cannot hide it in our houses because Elshers will come to know about it" he starts driving. The car's movements are insanely smooth. "How will they know?"

"There is a common bird here that are attracted to these things, if they smell this bracelet, they're gonna chirp so much that they'll know" then he points outside the window "Look, that's the bird, we call them Olynx"

I look at the bird for a while and say "That's a sparrow" "No it's an Olynx here"

I want to ask them where are we going to hide it, but I'm a scramble-head right now. I'm really tired and stressed. I came here to escape my problems, but I ended up creating more. I felt like a murderer after killing that kid, and now I feel like a criminal. I don't even know who that kid was.

Why did she vandalize our restaurant? Was it a coincidence that she came in front of my car? I suppose she was a homeless kid, because no parents would let they're child go out of the house at late night alone.

But what bothers me the most is that, where was her body after the accident? I'm pretty sure she was dead when I woke up. Were Trevor and Blair lying to me? But why would they?

The best part of all this is that now I don't need to worry about it, because it doesn't matter anymore.

Sage

"So this is your room" he says as I sit on the fluffiest bed I've ever felt. First I kept thinking why am I staying at his house? But then I assumed that, Valerie wasn't a person so she often faded away, mostly at night. Until I afford to get a place of my own, I guess I'll be staying here. This is so exciting.

I met Reagan's parents. At first, they weren't so welcoming. Not that they were rude, they seemed unsure about me. But at dinner time, we had lots of fun. We got along easily. They told me they love my personality. I found out that Ellery is the odd one out here. Everyone is goofy and soft hearted, but she is contrary.

"Thanks a lot. I can't express how happy I am. I never thought I'll be so happy after the accident and…"

"You got into an accident?" he interrupts. Dang, I mentioned it. Now I have to answer his questions. "How and when?"

I sit comfortably on the bed "Well, last night. Before coming here, I was in the hospital. I just lost my balance while driving, that's it"

He sits down "Is that really it? You're sweating" I touch my forehead and realize that I really am sweating. Thoughts of that accident keep scaring me. "Yeah um, it was really intimidating. It was raining that time and it made it scarier. But what scares me the most is that I accidently hit a little girl" he raises his eyebrows and asks "Did she die?"

I nod "I feel so bad about it. She looked only about ten years old. But the terrifying part is that, Blair told me there was no other body other than me. I'm pretty sure she died, then how did she just disappear?"

He stares at me. I don't understand what type of stare is that. It doesn't look like he's confused; it looks like he just realized something. He gulps and asks "Can you describe her appearance?" he says that in a deep and heavy voice.

I wait a few seconds before replying "Well, she was covered with a hood and had freckles…" he gasps. I stop describing more because I think he knows what he needed to. "Is something wrong?" I place my hand on his shoulder.

He was looking down on his knees. He shakes his head "Nothing important" then he looks up at me with his *dimply smile* "You have a lot to catch up on" then he gives me a side hug and stands up to leave. But we both flinch when there is a really loud and hard knock on the door.

It doesn't sound like there is an angry person on the door, because they only knocked thrice in once. But it was loud. Before we even left the room to have a look on whom it is, Reagan's parents had the door. When we came to look, I saw four people already standing inside the house. One of them looks like a really elegant man, while all the others are literally guards. I think I know who it is.

While we saw Mr. Knox talking to him, I asked Reagan "Don't tell me *that's* Truett" he nods in agreement. Truett is way more attractive than I thought. His skin is flawless, and my favorite part about him right now is his dark black hair that he had set up, but a few strands of his hair were on his eyes, that he never pushed back. His face looked like he never smiled.

"What sort of a lamebrain…Oh" Ellery says, coming out of her room. "Prince Truett, you startled me"

"It doesn't bother us" he says. His voice suits his face so much. "Do we have a problem?" Reagan says stepping ahead. "We came to know about a missing child" the way he said *child* was so cool. He pronounced it like *cha-yald*. "But that's not it," he says holding his hands behind him and raising his chin up "We were also told that, the child escaped this world, *without a wristlet of cover*" I could see Reagan swallow a lump that formed in his throat.

"I think you have a misunderstanding" Reagan finally says. "Oh yeah? Reagan, my friend, don't act like we don't know you. We both were good friends, weren't we?" his voice was soft and friendly here, but then his voice turned husky "Where is Aera?"

I look up at Reagan, waiting for him to respond. But he just kept quite. And then, Truett's attention falls on me. "Valerie, you look way more beautiful today, and way more *full of emotions*. What's so special today?" he knows. I know he knows. But I don't know how to react. "Start searching" he says that while piercing me with his looks. And the guards start searching the house.

Holy crapping biscuits.

Reagan looks at Ellery and signs something. "Truett! You know, it's so late already, you could have visited us tomorrow" it seems like she's distracting him.

"It's *Prince* Truett," he says "And we do not care if it's late or early"

"Well, *Prince Truett,* do I look like I care if you give crap about anything. No. You are disrupting our slumber" she responds back. I don't understand what's going on. Who is Aera? "Reagan, what is going on?" I turn around to face him, but he isn't there. Where'd he go?

As soon as Truett turned away from Ellery, keeping an eye on his guards, I ask her "What is he doing?"

She holds my wrist and pulls me away from Truett. "He is our *jerky* prince. Aera is our younger sister and she has been missing, perhaps entered your world without a wristlet of cover. That is forbidden. I'll tell that story later. So that's why he is here looking for her…and your bracelet" I gasp. Then I whisper back "I'll go to prison?"

"You were about to, but Reagan is gone" I don't understand. Then realization hit me. He took my bracelet and he's gone. "Where does he plan to take it" that's when she gulps "No idea. I told him not to leave, but now he's in trouble. Firstly, he's alone so late, and if Truett finds him, *he* would be in prison instead of you"

I'm literally a black cat. I left my messed up life in Houston, and I'm messing my life here. And now I can't even return back to Houston.

Oh my God, I'm so selfish. Ellery was right, I just find a way to run away from my responsibilities. Reagan is in trouble. "Lets go find him"

"Are you nuts?" "Are *you* nuts? You plan to leave your brother in trouble? You lost your sister Aera, and now you want to lose your brother too? You're a narcissistic" as soon as I say that, Truett comes from behind, which makes me startled.

"Luckily, we found nothing today. But unluckily, Aera is going to prison tomorrow. Good night and, sweet dreams"

"Bitter nightmares" Ellery mumbles to herself. Then Truett and his people finally leave. I run back to my room to find my bracelet, hoping that Ellery is again *intimidating me for her divertissement.*

I can hear Ellery explaining stuff to her parents. I can't find the bracelet, Ellery is right. Reagan is totally in trouble. I sit on my bed with my head in my hands. Ellery enters the room when I look up at her. She crosses her arms and says "I'm not a narcissistic, lets go"

She just says that and turns around. Where are we supposed to go? "You coming?" she asks without looking. I stand up as a response. "Where are we going?"

She just sighs "You do a lot interrogation, don't you?" she says that putting two water bottles in a bag "You have the right to, though. We'll be proceeding to pay a call to a greenwood"

"You mean forest?" forests must be common here. "Reagan's objective must be to fling your bracelet in the pink cataract" she adds some more things in the bag and zips it. She faces me and realizes I didn't understand her. She rolls her eyes "The pink cataract is actually a waterfall, perhaps a portal to your world. It's guarded by guards so no one can escape but, how hard would it be to just toss a wristlet. He might be punched and fined, nothing more." Then she tilts her head towards the door. "I already told mom and dad that we're leaving"

I'm astonished how their parents are okay with letting their teenage kid go out in a forest at late night. "They allowed you to do so?"

"Me and Aera are foster kids" and that's all she says. That explains pretty much everything. She opens the door to leave when I say "Ellery, it's so dangerous and it's so late"

"If we leave tomorrow, we won't be able to make it" I stare at her for a second or two, then nod. I just want to save Reagan. He's taking this risk for me, then I'll risk it for him.

She smirks and says "I'm a noceur and a dendrophile anyways. And I love werifesteria" I didn't understand anything she said, but I guess she meant she's okay with this adventure.

We've been walking towards the opposite direction of the village for about fifteen minutes. She hasn't said anything, but leading me. That's when the number of trees starts to increase. She hasn't even told me if we've reached or not, but I assume this is the greenwood.

It's so dark that I can't have a proper look at it, but I've tripped twice. "Are you going to tell me where are we?" I said after tripping for the third time. "You never asked me. Oh well, we've entered the woodland thirty minutes ago" wow, I didn't realize that we've been walking for about an hour now. "Should we be scared that we're deep in the forest now?" she nods.

She nods a yes.

How can she be so chill about it? "Be careful and keep an eye on the trees, a Ferex might jump on you"

"What is a Ferex?"

She sides eyes me. "I've studied about your world. In your world, Ferex are called wild donkeys, I guess" Donkey? Why would a donkey jump on me from the trees? "Do you mean wild *Monkeys*"

"Most probably, yes"

Yesterday I was sitting on my couch and reading my old journal, and today I'm wandering in a forest, scared for my life. I thought I was going to get a pleasant life here, but it's all the opposite. "Valerie watch your step!" she shouted. Before I could absorb what she was trying to say, I felt like I missed a step.

I stumbled and fell from a hill, why the next thing I know, I'm inside water. And I don't know how to swim. It's a running river. My eyes are closed and I can't see Ellery. I can only hear the river.

I try my best to stay on top of the water. I finally, faintly see Ellery running in the direction of the river. The river was loud, yet I think I heard her say "Hold on!"

Reagan

I have to apologize to Sage as soon as I get back home. I feel so bad for her. She just got here and she already feels like a criminal. Whatever happens, I'm not letting her go to prison. But I know for a fact that Truett would do anything to get revenge from me.

I was young at that time when Truett and I were classmates. King Jasper didn't sent Truett in Royal school or didn't homeschooled him. They believed that if Truett went with ordinary people, he will love us more. But the plan didn't go accordingly.

Truett started bullying others a lot. But he always got away with it. Once I got into a verbal fight with him which started his hatred for me. But we even got into a physical fight. Well, it wasn't a fight because apparently, I was beaten up. That happened when his crush asked me to prom. It wasn't her or my mistake because first of all, she didn't know Truett liked her. And I apologized to her because I decided to take Valerie to prom with a hope I might start liking her. But she wasn't as special as Sage.

I thought Sage will be just like Valerie, but when I was forcefully sent to the other world, I was so lonely and helpless. I thought I was stuck there forever. Little did I know that Sage would be such a blessing. When she first saw me in her dream, I tried my best to let her know about here, but I ended up saying *not to come up to me*.

I thought I would ruin her well made up life. I was so confused as to what to do. As Reagan, I saw how much she loved Blair and Trevor, and I didn't want her to leave them. But as Clyder, I wanted her with me. I wanted to see her smile because of me everyday. I wanted to be each others personal diary every single day.

When I first saw her in her restaurant, I noticed how shock she was. I just wanted to hug her and tell her everything. But I wanted to stay longer, even if I had to pretend I don't know her.

And about Truett, he hates me. He is really arrogant, haughty and selfish. He thinks he's already the ruler and doesn't tolerate anyone standing against him. So that's why he hates me. And he would never *ever* leave troubling me.

I always act fearless in front of him, but he intimidates me. The power that he holds is just, terrifying. He could just kick me out of the country.

He is a really well mannered and well educated man. He's always organized and knows what he does. I wish he never hated me.

I'm sitting under two tall and extensive trees that are a little bend towards each other that gives good shelter. If I didn't ran away from there, this would be the last day of Sage with us for some good long years.

I don't want her to end up like Aera.

The only way I could save her is throwing this bracelet in the pink cataract. But as far as I know Truett, he's going to be here. He loves seeing me suffer.

Not only will he seize Sage, he will take good care of me. But he won't be able to find me till tomorrow morning, so I'm good for now. But tomorrow he's going to navigate me easily.

Sage

"You are such a chowder head" Ellery says while trying to light up a fire. I was all wet from my head to toe. I don't even know how she saved me. I almost thought I would drown to death.

I couldn't stop shivering, it is icy cold here. When she finally lights it up, it finally felt warmer. "Did rubbing rocks really work?" I ask. She holds up a lighter "I used this"

"Why do you have a lighter in your pocket? You smoke?"

She sits down facing me "I would love to buy cigarettes one day. But first, let me get a career" I rub my palms and make them face the fire to heat them up. It felt like my hands are ice cubes and they are starting to melt. "You know, smoking isn't cool, it kills"

"Humans are born to die one day. I'm not a fan of life, it's evil"

The clothes are all wet, but I can't change because I have nothing to wear. I guess I'm gonna be sick. "Where will we spend the night?" I ask. She sniffs and says "Here"

We're literally in the middle of a forest, where I hear owls. "What do you mean here?"

"I'm pretty sure you speak English and understand what I mean"

We sit in silence for a minute. Then she reaches for her bag and takes out two small blankets and hands one to me. "I'm shivering with cold, and you didn't mind it? Why didn't you hand it to me earlier?"

"You didn't ask"

I groan. I'm literally stuck with her. I wrap it around me. She doesn't have any sleeping bag, I can tell because she has already spread the blanket and lay on it. "This isn't safe" I said.

"This forest only has wild Ferex and no other creatures that'll eat us up, if you wonder. The Ferexes might just spring on your face, rousing you. And if that's ridiculous to you, you are more than welcome to pull an all-nighter." She keeps her palms under her head and stares at the sky.

It's utterly silence here. Just the owls making the *goo-goo* sound. It so calm here. If I add up all the moments I had from yesterday, this would be the most serene one.

"I suppose you had oneirataxia" she says after few minutes of silence. "What's that?"

She turns to my side, resting her head in one hand "Oneirataxia, when you are unable to find the difference between fantasy and reality"

I smile. "Well," I sigh "I always doubted my existence though. And I always thought that, there might be another world somewhere" I bring my palms to my cheeks to warm them up "When I first saw your brother, I never thought so deep about stuff. Now I know why I felt a sudden and weird bond with him. And today I don't even know where he's sleeping"

She inhales deeply "Your Limerence towards him is winsome. But actually, I never took a shine to Valerie. I always called Reagan a chucklehead because he never lost hope for you. Aera liked you though" she looks back at the sky. I stare at her for a while.

"Do you miss her?"

She doesn't respond. I can already tell that she isn't the type of person who can express her emotions. "I don't know, we weren't really close" she said. She won't admit it, but I know she does. I spread my blanket and lay down, staring at the sky with her.

"I never liked my sister either. We always used to fight and we never got along. But even when we don't feel it, we do have a soft spot for them" maybe I shouldn't continue this topic. "So," I change the subject "Why did Aera enter my world?"

Ellery groans and says "Okay so, Aera, she was the quite kid of the class, and an Eccedentesiast. She was really creative, she loved singing and writing" I wish I could meet her, because she sings, and I play instrument. And she writes, and I read. We would become an amazing duo.

"She was writing a novel, well I guess it's unfinished and will never end. Anyways, as I told you that we were foster kids, Mrs. Knox pressures me to study, like a lot. She wants me to study twenty four by seven. Once I got eighty nine percent on an exam, she grounded me for a week." Sounds so much like Ms. Darren.

"And about Aera, well she is just made for the house chores. She never gets to meet friends or celebrate events. Reagan once helped us sneak out but we were unsuccessful. It's only Reagan in the house who appreciates us." That made me like him even more. "Aera got in depression because of all this, and she believed that if she brought you here, everything would change. But she was too young to know about the wristlet of cover. One day at night, no one knows how but, she jumped in the pink cataract. She still hasn't returned and Truett's people might find her" and she doesn't say anything after that. But my mind starts yelling.

Why does nothing sound good? Have I met Aera? "How old was she?"

"Ten"

That moment I felt like a sharp knife carving my heart. My mind started repeating her name. *Aera. Aera. Aera.* A part of me wants to believe that it was all a coincidence.

I killed Aera? And Reagan knows it now because he asked me earlier. Oh my god this can't be true. Aera did that vandalizing on purpose so that I would notice her. *I killed her?*

And I suppose that Truett's people found her body, that's why she wasn't there. The thought about killing a kid already bothered me so much, but now it hurts. I killed Reagan's sister who thought I would make her life better. But instead I ended it. It's my fault. All of it. Every consequences I'm facing today, it's my entire fault. It's *me* who is the villain of my life.

Ellery isn't looking at me so she doesn't see my red eyes and trembling hands. "When did you come to know about the motive of your wristlet?" she asks, making me snap out of my thoughts. I breathe in deeply, hoping I don't have a mental breakdown. "Well," I don't really want to make it complicated by including the red book and all "Long story short, I found weird things in your brothers house and that made me question my mom about my wristlet. I had an argument with her then"

She turns towards me "What did you argue about?"

"About why she didn't tell me this earlier"

She curls her eyebrows and sits up "You fought your mom for that? Excuse me? You fought your mom because she loved you so much and was afraid to lose you?" she runs her hands through her hair "You should have hugged her and should be thanking her. Jeez!" and then she lays back down, going to sleep for good.

Now she made me feel more dreadful about myself. I'm such a piece of crap. She isn't wrong though. Maybe that's the problem, she's too brutally honest.

Reagan

I wake up with water sprinkling on me. I open my eyes to realize it's raining. My vision is blurry. The trees seem so unusual. Their shape is similar to humans and they are colorful. I rub my eyes and flinch when I see that there are real human beings standing in front of me.

And one of them is Truett.

He grabs my collar and lifts me up. "Did you sleep well?" he asks. He grabbed my collar so hard that it was difficult to talk or breathe. "Truett…" I hold his hand that is gripping my collar. He throws me on the ground with high force. "Hand us over the wristlet" he says looking down at me. He hasn't noticed the small cloth pouch I have in my hand.

"I don't have it"

"There is no use of lying to us" he yells at me. I yell back at him "Valerie has it not me!" then I point behind him. The second he turns around, expecting to see Valerie standing there, I run. I run without looking back.

The rain was very light, but it still made the path slippery. However, I managed to run. But I can't outrun Truett. He is a well trained Prince. I could feel him and his people running and yelling at me.

I kept telling myself "Don't look back, don't look back" but I was so terrified that I turned my head to look back. They were so close to me.

My legs started trembling. When I turned back around, I almost fell into a ravine.

My toes are on the edge and I feel like I'm going to lose my balance and fall into the deep ravine. And it happened, I lost my balance. I close my eyes, afraid to accept that it will never open now. I don't know how deep it is until my bones break and I lay on my blood.

But it wasn't happening. I open my eyes and realize that I didn't fell. Truett is holding my shirt from behind, preventing me from falling. He pulls back, but grips my hair. He raises his hand, probably asking for the bracelet "We could tear you apart and chop you into pieces if we wanted. Do not risk it, Reagan"

I don't have a choice.

I don't...

I hand him over the cloth pouch, and he releases my hair. He smirks, taking the pouch "Glorious. Now please, we want you to bring your Valerie for dinner at my castle. In the *castle prison*. Tell her that we offer her a free room in the prison for ten years. *She doesn't have a choice*" I know that he saw me gulp. "We'll give you a ride home, buddy"

"I'm fine" and I just walk away from there. Defeat tastes so bitter.

I hear him open the cloth bag and as soon as he does, once again, I run. Does he think that I'm an idiot? I knew he will get me somehow. So, *I had the bracelet in my pocket.*

He didn't left me though. He was still chasing me. I don't know how long will it take for him to lose me.

Sage

I felt like someone was pouring water on me, so I yelled "Trevor stop!! I'm awake now!" I open my eyes to find Ellery staring at me. "There ain't any Trevor here. It's raining come get shelter" she moves under a tree, so do I.

I totally forgot that I'm not in Texas. I'm not heavily wet because the rain isn't really heavy. I saw Ellery fondly looking at the sky. She wasn't smiling but, her face says so much. "You love rain, don't you?"

She turns towards me "Of course. I'm a Pluviophile" I'm not sure what that means. She looks back at the rain "My favorite thing about it is petrichor"

"And what does it mean?"

"The smell of earth after rain"

I nod in agreement. "What about you? You woke up annoyed because of the water on you" I stare at the ground for a few seconds before speaking "I don't know. The last time I was in rain, it was a horrible disaster. I don't blame the rain for it"

"How munificence of you"

I look around, finally getting a view of the forest. Choked by its own overgrown branches, the greenwood resembled a sprawling fortress, barricading the earth from the warmth of the sun and the blue of the sky.

A carpet of fine evergreen needles covered the ground, perfuming the clearing with a pungent yet sweet scent. It isn't scary as I thought.

"I used to love rain too, I wish that night never occurred, and I wouldn't put you guys in trouble. My whole life, I thought it was me who was the victim. I went through a lot. But I wanted a better life so much that I made everyone in my life suffer"

She looks at me for a while, then says "You aren't a bad person" she sighs "You never meant to do anything bad to anyone" I shake my head to a no. "It's easy to say it Ellery"

She crosses her arms "Okay, name me all the person who suffered because of you" I stare at her for a minute, thinking very deeply.

"Trevor, Blair, Amy, My mom and Reagan" I could also name Emma, because she *almost* suffered because of me. But I won't call Aera, even though she suffered the most because of me. "Are you sorry for them?"

I nod. "Then that's it. It's more than enough. It's better than blaming yourself"

I chew on my bottom lip, roaming my eyes around. That's when I hear someone running. I thought I'm going crazy, but I saw Ellery looking around as well. "You hear that?' I nod.

That's when we both saw Reagan running. Ellery grabs my wrist and runs towards his direction. Reagan didn't notice us yet. She releases my hand mid way. "Why is he running?" I ask. That very moment we heard more footsteps running.

"Truett is here" she says. My heart starting hammering faster. If he gets caught, we're all done for sure.

None of them has noticed both of us, which is actually good. That's when I see Truett throwing a knife at Reagan, which directly hits his arm. He groans out of the agony. We have to do something before Truett catches him up.

Reagan ran for five minutes after being stabbed, and now he looks like he's gonna collapse because of the pain. His shirt is already soaked in blood.

"Listen," Ellery says "Take Reagan and run, I'll stop Truett"

"But you-" "Forget about me, just go!"

She turns her way and bumps really hard into Truett that made him trip and fall. And on the other side, Reagan was holding his bleeding arm and was on his knees. I run up to him and without saying a word, I pick him up and help him walk out of there.

The trees were getting bigger and they blocked the view. The last thing I saw before leaving was Truett grabbing Ellery's hair with extreme anger and rage in his eyes. He didn't saw us leave.

We walked far enough, and I came to the view of a beautiful pink waterfall. The guards that stand before it can't see us right now. "Reagan, we've reached the pink cataract"

"Sage," he said. I make him sit down near a tree. "Does it pain bad?"

"No, it doesn't pain at all. Why are you here alone?"

"I'm here with Ellery. And that doesn't matter. Give me the bracelet. Once we throw it, they'll have no proof to arrest me"

I notice his pocket and take out the bracelet. As soon as I stand up, he pulls my arms and made me sit back down. He holds my arms and looks me in the eyes. "You have to go" he says. I tilt my head, signing that I don't get it. "You have to go back to your world"

There was pain in his eyes. Tears were flowing out of them, but none of them brought pain out of him. I felt my heart shattering. I felt my whole self shattering. It's like his words were arrows that pierced my heart.

I got goose bumps when he said that. "Reagan but..." he holds my cheeks with his palms "Sage, it isn't safe here. Listen to me and please return back. You won't regret it"

He was all wet, and his arm just wouldn't stop bleeding. I don't know how to react. All I could do is cry.

"I don't want to..." I sob. "Hey, it's okay. Trust me, I had the best time of my life with you. I just wanted to meet you and I did. I'm okay with living without you but I cannot see you suffer here"

He presses his forehead with mine and closes his eyes. I could feel both of our faces wet with tears "Promise me you'll never forget Clyder, promise me Sage..."

I shake my head "Never..." he pulls himself back and holds my shoulder "Always remember that, time heals all wounds, okay?" he lifts my wrist and takes the bracelet to put it back on.

This is it, *this* is my fate. I want to hate my fate and life so much, but I'm so happy to know that my fate gave me a person like Reagan. Even though I don't deserve him at all.

This is how our story ends, everything ends here. From the moment I saw him, my eyes always searched him everywhere. And now that I have his hands in mine, I have to let go of him, all of a sudden.

The last look he gives me was full of love, appreciation and warmth. He looked at me the way no one ever did. And with that, I put back the wristlet...and fade away.

I never dreamed of this ending with Reagan. The moment I came into this world, I thought I might live my best life, it never happened. But he knew what was best for me, even though it broke him. However, whatever happens, it will be hard as hell to forget his blue eyes filled with ocean.

THE END

Epilogue

"The truck is loaded!" Trevor informs me. "All the orders are done! Let it go!"

Blair enters with a carry bag and places it on the counter "I brought you tacos. Thought you'll be hungry" she smiles and picks up her phone that was buzzing since she entered. "They are the new ones that came in our restaurant. I swear they're so damn tasty" she said before leaving.

It's been two years since that incident, and it has started to feel like my life was always as perfect as it is right now. Reagan was a golden retriever, after I left that world, nothing went wrong.

I see another customer enter. "Hey! Welcome to my store, how may I help you?"

"Oh my god, I didn't expect to meet the owner right here" they said. "Well, I love interacting with my customers so yeah"

"Great! So can we get started with body lotions please? And then cleansers" I call an employee and tell her to lead the customers. I always dreamed of it, but I never imagined being the owner of my own company, one of the best and most famous skincare and cosmetics store.

I remember struggling with naming it, but once I left that world, I was damn sure about it. More customers enter as my employee greet them "Hi! Welcome to *Clyders*"

Clyders and Sunbread Woods are nominated for the best businesses of Texas. If that wasn't enough, I even got my own apartment.

Well, Clyder didn't lie when he told me that, whatever I'll name my company, it would be amazing.

"Wow" Amy enters the store. She hasn't been here for a long time. The last time she saw the store was when it was small and unpopular. So she's obviously astonished to see it crowded and extremely bright.

She walks up to me with a smile "I knew you could do it, I never doubted you"

I look down at my feet, not knowing how to respond. I still haven't formed a friendly relationship with Amy. And I don't think I ever will. "Give me few moments" saying that, I leave the store to my car. *My own car.*

I start driving without sitting idle in the car for even a moment. It was night time and the city glittered like a thousand diamonds, an oasis of light in the darkness. I kept driving for twenty minutes till I reach my destination.

I jump out of my car and run on the sand. I stand before sparkling water that had the moon's reflection on it. Last time I was here, I had a mental breakdown and I cursed at my fate.

But the case is so different now. Like a bud opening in the spring, happiness blossomed within me, its sweet fragrance eradicating the fetid decay of the previous season.

Even though they say that time heals all wounds, the scars are still there. But actually, I learned that time doesn't heal any wound. It just teaches us how to live with it.

But there is still a handful of sadness somewhere deep within my heart that refuses to show up. My happiness covers it so well that I can't even feel it. Sometimes I think that it is the frustration of Amy's presence. It is but not all of it.

Maybe it's the sadness of Reagan's absence. The bond that was created with him was strange. Even though I just imagined all of it, those were the best moments of my life.

Acknowledgments

The story didn't have this ending when I first decided to write it. When I planned out this novel, Amy's role ended after she stabbed Sage. But I felt bad for leaving Amy behind so I found the perfect way to get her back.

The fun fact about the story is that Reagan Knox was made and formed AFTER I created Clyder. How funny is that? But that doesn't mean I had Clyder for nothing. I had something else planned for him. But I never let that happened because it was so cruel and unfair for both Clyder and Sage.

Reading is just a habit and hobby for some people, but few people like me have a whole different world inside it. We read it to escape this real world and jump into the fictional world of books. That's what my story was about. Just like we bookworms escape reality with the help of books, Sage escaped her heartbreaking reality.

To all the people who found this book and read it, I thank you a lot. This is my first ever novel and I was so excited to write it in the whole writing process.

First of all I will love to thank my father, Khushnood Akhtar, who always believed in me and my writing skills. And my mother, Farzana Ghani, who was by my side all the time. This book wouldn't exist without them.

I want to thank my cousin, Inaaya, because even though Blair didn't have a huge role in the book, she did, in my life.

I don't know how to start. Well, I went through a hard time in 2021, where I was completely hopeless about everything. I had this small YouTube channel, where I remember I posted a long paragraph explaining about my problems and my anxiety. About an hour later, I saw all of my friends reply stuff like *"I know right, I have this too" "I can relate" "I suffer like this too"* and more where they were just telling how THEY suffer like me.

But I still remember what she texted me, *"Hey, I just saw your post, is something wrong? You can talk to me if you're comfortable"* these were her exact words.

It is such a small thing, but it made me cry so much that I had to screenshot it. It meant the world to me because I've never heard anyone else say it to me before. I texted her back as if I didn't care, but I remember this very thing till today. Not just this, she was literally my therapist. And the fact that we meet each other once in two-three years is mind blowing.

That's not the only reason I'm acknowledging her. She is the main reason I got into reading and writing once again after years of giving up.

Thank you Sidra, Jahnvi and Ariza for always hyping me up.

And thank you to everyone who was in the process of publishing this book. I can't thank you guys enough.